How Shall They Hear?

The Art of Effective Biblical Preaching

How Shall They Hear?

The Art of Effective Biblical Preaching

*Featuring Interviews and Sermon Outlines of
Dr. Herbert H. Barber and Dr. James M. Boice*

Aldwin Ragoonath

Unless otherwise indicated, all Scripture verses quoted are from *The Greek New Testament*, Kurt Aland et al., eds. Printed by the United Bible Society in Stuttgart, Germany (Wurttemberg Bible Society, [1966] 1968).

How Shall They Hear?: The Art of Effective Biblical Preaching
by Aldwin Ragoonath
ISBN 0-88270-689-6
Library of Congress Catalog Card Number: 96-84852
Copyright © 1996 by BRIDGE-LOGOS *Publishers*

Published by:
BRIDGE-LOGOS *Publishers*
North Brunswick Corporate Center
1300 Airport Road, Suite E
North Brunswick, NJ 08902

Table of Contents

Foreword...vii

Acknowledgments..xiii

1.) Effective Biblical Preaching...........................1

2.) Preaching Models: Barber and Boice.........27

3.) Practical Implementation of the
   Principles of Textual Expository
   Preaching...63

Appendixes..89

Foreword

Our time has been described in many ways. It has been called the "age of sensation," referring to experience as normative. Hugh Mackay refers to it as the "age of anxiety" and the "age of redefinition."

People have an inner fear about the future. Living in modernity has caused many dislocations. The rate of change is so fast that people move from one dislocation to another, always gasping for breath to catch up in a never-ending process—and eventually losing their bearings and sense of purpose.

However we describe our time, we recognize three trends that contribute to modern man feeling, if not becoming, "a rimless zero floating in the sea of nothingness." Churches cannot disengage themselves from these realities. They provide the context in which pastors are to shape their ministries and direct their messages.

From the absolute to the relative.

We live in an increasingly secularistic society. Secularism leads to pluralism. Pluralism leads to relativism. Simply stated, we experience the loss of authority, the undermining of the Bible as God's absolute Word to man. David Wells wrote of this in his *No Place For Truth*. Reginald W. Bibby once said that Canadians deserve to be nominated as "champions of choices." The problem is each choice is as relevant as the other, leading to a paralysis wherein "one tolerates everything and seldom takes a position on anything."

From depravity to determinism.

In the past, the church has had no problem affirming that the root cause of the "twilight of western civilization" is sin. As Paul declares, "all have sinned." Today, man rejects his depravity and sin as a category but reasons that deviant behaviors are determined by one's environment. Man is not a sinner but a product of societal factors that affect his life.

> If there is no sin, then there is no guilt.
>
> If there is no guilt, then there is no need for atonement.
>
> If there is no sin, then there is no need for a Savior.

Determinism deals a death blow to the religion of the soul. Yet, the bankruptcy of the secularistic-relativistic alternative can lead to a revival or open the door wide to the Gospel message.

From theology to therapy.

The move from theology to therapy logically follows relativism and determinism. Our time has become the age of psychology. We cite Freud, et al., to probe into the inner psyche of man in order to give him purpose and meaning. The psychosis of our time has reached epidemic proportions. As Peter Berger, Brigitte Berger, and Hansfried Kellner point out, "the individual can no longer recognize himself in his anonymized identity" and needs "emotional management" as part of this "psychological engineering."

From the loss of authority, to the loss of sin, to the loss of meaning! And these are the issues that biblical preaching has to deal with.

Against such a context, I find Dr. Aldwin Ragoonath's book, *How Shall They Hear?,* a most engaging work. It is like a fresh wind that gently blows into the suffocating atmosphere of society—and even churches. It is a book not just to read, but to reflect upon. It is biblical and practical. It is intellectual and experiential. It is a book with a *telic,* or purpose. It strongly advocates sermonic order— homiletics. Let me help plumb the depth of riches that awaits the readers.

First, Dr. Ragoonath convincingly allows the Bible to define preaching and traces its history from synagogue preaching to the New Testament model of Christ—and then to the relevant and logical preaching of contemporaries like Dr. Herbert H. Barber of Calvary Temple in Winnipeg, Canada, and Dr. James M. Boice of Tenth Presbyterian Church in Philadelphia, Pennsylvania. But his commitment to textual/expository preaching is, foremost, anchored on *sola scriptura*, on the "conviction that the Bible is God's Word." The Word of God is the authority in matters of life and faith. He quotes Dr. Barber, saying, "believing in the inerrancy of scripture is primary in being a good expositor." Where there is no Word, the people will perish.

Secondly, Dr. Ragoonath gives us a scholarly analysis of the structure of expository preaching. Here he draws from the style of many prominent and successful expositors and, importantly, from his own experience. He knows and practices the art of textual/expository preaching. He covers the ground thoroughly for the pastor who is serious about preaching. He deals with planning sermons for the year, developing sermons with examples of sermon analysis, and includes a wide-ranging bibliography on preaching. But he reveals his heart when he repeatedly insists that biblical preaching is "Christocentric preaching." As a litmus test in his sermons, he would ask: "Where is Christ in the sermon?" His overriding thesis is that "Christocentric preaching must always point to Jesus." Pluralism legitimizes expressions and choices. Choices have consequences. The offer of the Christ-choice is the most significant message to modern man today for Christ is God's final and last Word to man.

Thirdly, Dr. Ragoonath believes that pastors should be prepared "to spend a lifetime in one congregation" to really know the people and to allow for expository preaching book by book. He insists that "excellent preaching is not a coincidence, but "a product of academic excellence and prayer—and hard work." His life is an antidote to the anonymized life of modern man. It is one with clear sense of purpose, one that lifts man to worship the Divine. In the same way, throughout the book you find a pastor consumed with the care of his congregation—desiring to see them grow in the faith. The meaning and purpose of life is in Christ—not just to know Him but to grow in Him. The author is clear on this prescription when he speaks of preaching as teaching.

Reviewing the book as a tool for preaching gave me so much help. Reading the book through the heart of Dr. Ragoonath brought me renewal; to recognize the sacred trust of expounding the Word to hearers, to rededicate myself to the noble task of biblical preaching which is textual/expository preaching. As James Daane once said:

> Only in the church is the Proclaimed also the Proclaimer. It was to those commissioned to preach His Word that Jesus said, "He that heareth you heareth me; and he that despiseth you despiseth me; and he that despiseth me

despiseth him that sent me" (Luke 10:16). This is the agony and the glory, the power and foolishness, the high honor and awesome responsibility of the Christian minister. The Christian ministry functions on the borderline between the cross and the resurrection, between heaven and hell. This frontier is no place for the faint-hearted; those who have little faith in their message and its power do not belong to the pulpit."

This is one book I am happy to recommend to pastors, missionaries, and lay leaders who desire to preach the Word in season and out of season.

Dr. Agustin B. Vencer, Jr.
International Director
World Evangelical Fellowship

Acknowledgments

I want to thank Dr. Joe Pippa, Director of the Doctor of Ministry program at Westminster Theological Seminary in California, for accepting me into the program and for his personal help and supervision. I am also grateful to the faculty who helped and taught me, especially Dr. J. Adams (Professor Emeritus) and Dr. Dennis Johnson (Academic Dean). All of these men helped sharpen my tools, enabling me to become a better preacher of the Gospel.

My thanks to Mr. William Schroder, M.A., of Winnipeg, Canada, a retired high school and Bible school teacher and editor of a German newspaper who has become a personal friend. He has labored long hours to edit and re-edit my work many times over. Without his help, this book would have been almost impossible.

I am grateful to the board and members of Agape Chapel, Winnipeg, Canada, who gave me time to pursue my studies.

To my wife, Rubena, and two beautiful daughters, Sharla and Christa, who helped in typing my manuscript; thank you all for your love and encouragement.

And to our great God and Savior Jesus Christ, who gave me the desire and strength to complete this program, be all the praise and glory.

****1****

Effective Biblical Preaching

What is biblical preaching?

I can hear you saying, "Look it up in a homiletical text book" or "Ask a successful pastor of a large church and you'll get a clear definition of preaching."

The problem with the first suggestion is that sometimes the answer might be lopsided. The writer may emphasize one point of preaching from the Scriptures, or he may emphasize only his interests. If the writer is interested in modern forms of communication, he may emphasize communication—if he is interested in logic, he will emphasize logic.

The problem with the second suggestion is that the answer is too often pragmatic—it is dependent upon successful preachers to define preaching. If a man is successful, his method becomes the measuring stick to define biblical preaching. He may be an effective preacher but not necessarily a biblical preacher.

In this chapter, we will look to the Bible to define biblical preaching. The Bible speaks for itself and will guide us as we seek to acquire an understanding of biblical preaching. It is imperative that we obtain a clear understanding of biblical preaching before we look at our two preaching model's suggestions for utilizing textual/expository preaching because, above all else, we want to make sure we are biblically correct.

Looking at what the Bible describes as biblical preaching will assist us in developing a definition. We will look at the similarities between the synagogue service and the New Testament service, at the New Testament words that describe preaching and the purpose of preaching, and at the great preachers' interpretation of preaching.

Biblical preaching is textual/expository in nature.

Pastoral preaching should be textual/expository in nature. Pastoral preaching should not be topical. Topical sermons run the risk of allowing a pastor to preach his own words and ideas. This method itself does not bind the preacher to the Scriptures as the authority for what is preached.

For example, a pastor may preach about "husbands" and obtain various Scriptures to show how husbands should behave, what husbands should and should not do, but he may not necessarily be scriptural.

Textual exposition means that a pastor may preach from one text or one portion of a text—from a whole chapter, a few verses of a chapter or a verse. The important requirement is that there is one complete thought-unit throughout the sermon.

In textual/expository preaching, a pastor preaches from a text as the guarantee of the truth. In topical preaching, he generally preaches about the text as the springboard for his comments. In topical preaching, a pastor may say whatever he wants to say about a topic and still feel safely assured that he is preaching God's Word. In textual/expository preaching, a pastor is confined to preaching from the text and about the text. In this way, he is assured that he is preaching the mind of Christ.

The preceding is only part of my definition of textual/expository preaching. As I develop my ideas in this chapter, you will get a clearer definition of what is meant by textual/expository preaching.

There are five reasons why I am convinced that pastoral preaching should be textual/expository in nature:

1. The history of Old Testament preaching verifies that textual/expository preaching was the method used at that time.

The first type of preaching recorded in the Bible is prophetic preaching.[1] For example, Noah was a preacher of righteousness, Elijah and Elisha preached to Israel, Isaiah and Jeremiah warned Israel to repent and turn to God.

While prophetic preaching continues today, another type of preaching evolved with the synagogue movement. This type of preaching was of a textual/expository nature. The synagogue movement was born while the children of Israel were in captivity and the need arose to worship God and study His Word.

3

During this time, the Jews met on the Sabbath for worship, prayer, and the study of God's Word. Usually at these gatherings someone would read from a portion of the Old Testament Scriptures and then translate, interpret, and apply what was read. This process became a sermon and was, in essence, textual/expository preaching.

Ezra's preaching is a good example of textual/expository preaching taking place outside the synagogue. Allow me to relate the incident again.

The children of Israel had been in captivity in Babylon for seventy years and they returned to Jerusalem and Judah under Ezra, Nehemiah, and Zerubbabel. They were trying to rebuild the city walls. The incident in Nehemiah, chapter eight, describes for us a public service. In this public service, the Scriptures (the Law) were read and explained.

> *So they read from the book, from the law of God, translating to give the sense so that they understood the reading.* (Nehemiah 8:8, AMP)

Ezra had to read from the Hebrew Scriptures, and then translate and apply them to the congregation in their language. In the above incident, we have some of the basic ingredients for textual/expository preaching— translation, explanation, and application. What I see here is a development taking place. Prophetic preaching continues, and pastoral preaching evolves and becomes textual/expository preaching in nature. I also see here the same dynamics of textual/expository preaching that took place in the synagogue preaching. It appears that Ezra's style of preaching was borrowed from the synagogue concept of preaching.

2. Synagogue preaching was textual/expository in nature in the time of Jesus.

I will outline a synagogue service for you before I prove my point:

(i)   Thanksgiving or "blessing" spoken in connection (before and after) the Shema: "Hear, O Israel, the Lord our God, the Lord is one, and you shall love the Lord your God with all your heart, and with all your soul, and with all your might."

(ii)   Prayer, with response of "Amen" from the congregation.

(iii)   Reading of a passage from the Pentateuch (in Hebrew, followed by translation into Aramaic).

(iv)   Reading of a passage from the prophets (similarly translated).

(v)   Sermon or word of exhortation.

(vi)   The Benediction pronounced by a priest— to which the congregation repeated "Amen." When no priest was present, a closing prayer was substituted for the Benediction.[2]

The heart of the synagogue service was preaching that was textual/expository in character. Notice from the outline of the synagogue service in points three, four, and five, that the emphasis is on the written Word—the Old Testament Scriptures were read and translated. In point five, there is a word of exhortation or a sermon. This was usually done from the original language of the Bible. In the time of Jesus, it was from Hebrew to Greek or Aramaic.

The incident in Luke 4:16-21(KJV) is a good example of the dynamics of textual/expository preaching that went on in a synagogue service:

> *And he came to Nazareth, where he had been brought up: and, as his custom was, he went into the synagogue on the sabbath day, and stood up for to read.*
>
> *And there was delivered unto him the book of the prophet Esaias. And when he had opened the book, he found the place where it was written,*
>
> *The Spirit of the Lord is upon me, because he hath anointed me to preach the gospel to the poor; he hath sent me to heal the brokenhearted, to preach deliverance to the captives, and recovering of sight to the blind, to set at liberty them that are bruised,*
>
> *To preach the acceptable year of the Lord.*
>
> *And he closed the book, and he gave it again to the minister, and sat down. And the eyes of all them that were in the synagogue were fastened on him.*
>
> *And he began to say unto them, This day is this scripture fulfilled in your ears.*

Yngve Brilith, an outstanding homilitician, in his book *A Brief History of Preaching*,[3] outlines three things that he saw in this synagogue service when Jesus said, *This day is this scripture fulfilled in your ears.*

First, it was liturgical:

> Jesus' sermon was delivered within the context of the Jewish service.

Second, it was exegetical:

> Jesus spoke from a text . . .

Third, it was prophetic:

> *Today this Scripture has been fulfilled in your hearing.* The content of Jesus' preaching was summed up in this prophetic declaration, which retained the characteristic crisp, lapidary style of the oracles.

I like the point where Brilith emphasizes Jesus' sermon as being exegetical. In essence he is saying, "Jesus' sermon was textual/expository in nature."[4]

For Jesus' preaching to be exegetical, several things had to take place. The Scriptures had to be translated by the teacher from Hebrew to the known language—in Jesus' day it was Hebrew to Greek or Aramaic. The text had to be explained—what it meant in its context. The text was expounded—explaining what it meant and showing the relationship to other Scriptures. The text was applied to the current culture in a relevant form. This is textual exposition.

3. Jesus gave His approval of this practice of preaching by attending and taking part in the synagogue services.

Luke 4:16-21 is one example where Jesus attended synagogue services and took part. Another example is Luke 4:44 where Jesus continued the practice of synagogue preaching: *And He continued to preach in the synagogues of Galilee* (AMP). Luke 4:16 says it was His custom to do so. That means He did so weekly. He not only attended synagogue services, He regularly taught in the synagogues. Matthew 9:35 tells us that in Galilee He *went about all the cities and villages, teaching in their synagogues.* Mark 1:21 says He taught in the synagogue in Capernaum.

4.   The New Testament Christian service was consistent with the synagogue service—the Word of God was expounded in both of these services.

I demonstrated earlier that the preaching of the Word was central to the synagogue service. We see the same centrality of preaching the Word of God in the Christian service. In 1 Corinthians 14:26 (KJV), we read, *everyone of you hath a psalm, hath a doctrine, hath a tongue, hath a revelation, hath an interpretation* (see also Ephesians 5:19 and Colossians 3:16). Doctrine, tongue, revelation, and interpretation have to do with speaking the Word (see 2 Timothy 4:2). The centrality of preaching is seen in Acts 11:26 (KJV) where we read, *he brought him unto Antioch. And it came to pass, that a whole year they assembled themselves with the church, and taught much people* (KJV).

I make the assertion that the exposition of God's Word was textual in nature, based upon the fact that Jesus followed the synagogue concept of preaching. Jesus and the Apostles accepted the idea of synagogue preaching, and the similarity of New Testament preaching leads me to believe that the early Church followed the same order.

5. Most of the great preachers interpreted biblical preaching as textual/expository in nature.

To name a few of these notable preachers: Origen, Augustine, Chrysostom, Bernard of Clairvaux, John Wycliff, John Calvin.[5] These great preachers should be taken seriously because they were conventional church leaders. They kept the tradition of preaching alive. This especially becomes more convincing when most of the great preachers say the same thing: "Great preaching is textual/expository preaching."

8

In summary, biblical preaching should be textual/expository in nature because pastoral preaching has its roots in synagogue preaching that was textual/expository in nature. Jesus approved the practice of textual/expository preaching. The New Testament service was consistent with the Old Testament synagogue service where the Word of God was expounded. And finally, most great preachers interpreted biblical preaching as textual/expository in nature.

Having looked at the method of preaching, we will now look at six different New Testament Greek words that describe preaching—and discuss the methods of textual/expository preaching found in each.

Biblical preaching is in keeping with the New Testament words that describe preaching.

Kerussein

This word was first used in secular Greek to announce good news. In 197 B.C., it was used to announce the victory of the Romans over the Greeks in the Greek games. A year later, it was used to declare the autonomy of the Greeks.[6]

In the New Testament, *kerussein* came to be understood as a declaration and announcement of the good news of the Gospel. It means "to declare the kingdom of God." It is also used in pastoral preaching in a synagogue service as part of worship and teaching.[7] The emphasis of this word is on proclamation. Generally, when used that way, it means Jesus is being proclaimed as Savior and Lord. In the New Testament, the noun form, *keryx,* is found three times (1 Timothy 2:7; 2 Timothy 1:11; 2 Peter 2:5), and it always refers to the proclaiming of a divine event.

The nominal cognate, *kerygma*, occurs six times in the New Testament and always refers to the Gospel message. The verb, *kerussein,* occurs approximately 59 times in the New Testament and refers to declaring the good news of the Gospel.[8] Klaas Runia, in an article, "What is preaching according to the New Testament?", summarizes this word when he says:

> The way in which kerussein is used tells us that preaching is not only the proclamation of a saving event that once took place in the life, death and resurrection of Jesus Christ, but it is also the announcement to the listener that, when he believes in this Jesus Christ, he finds himself in the new situation of salvation brought about by Jesus. The proclamation of the event inaugurates the new state of affairs for the believing listener.[9]

Kerussein, then, means to declare the Gospel and to offer salvation. It is the proclamation of the good news. It is the imparting of salvation.[10] And when it is proclaimed with authority and power, signs and wonders accompany the evangelical message.[11]

As it pertains to preaching today, this word suggests that we should preach with authority when we announce and declare the Gospel. We should not preach apologetically—or preach as if the Gospel was subject to one's opinion and proclaiming it was merely sharing an opinion. Instead, we should declare that Jesus died for our sins and that we can have forgiveness through His name.

Euangelizesthai

In the New Testament, the root word of this word is *evangel*, which means the Gospel—the good news that Jesus died for our sins. The word "evangelist" comes from the same root idea and means one who preaches the Gospel to non-Christians. In a general sense, *euangelizesthai* means "to proclaim the good news", but it came to mean "to declare the gospel of salvation." It is almost synonymous with *kerussein*. These words are used interchangeably or even together, having their background in the Old Testament, especially in Isaiah 52:7 and 61:1-3.[12] *Kerussein* emphasizes the event, while *euangelizesthai* emphasizes that it is a joyful message.[13] Jesus refers to Isaiah 61:1-3 as referring to Himself and His disciples (Luke 4:18). *Euangelizesthai* is evangelistic preaching—also pastoral preaching in the sense that pastors should do the work of an evangelist. This is important because the children of our church members need to hear the Gospel, and non-Christians sometimes visit our churches. Believers also need to be reminded of the saving work of God in Christ Jesus.

Marturein

Marturein has its origin in the courtroom. It refers to the witness. A witness is a person who testifies about what he has personally seen or heard regarding a matter under investigation.[14] In the New Testament, the word includes the idea that one experiences something or knows something because it was taught by divine revelation or inspiration.[15] The Apostles preached only what they were taught or had experienced.[16] They were true to what they had been taught, had seen, had heard, and had experienced under the ministry of Christ. They were true to the teachings of the death and resurrection of Christ. Since we have not experienced firsthand what they experienced, preaching today needs to be true to the Word of God— true to the apostolic tradition of teaching what they had experienced.[17]

Didaskein

Didaskein means "to teach; to deliver didactic discourses (Matthew 4:23); to discharge the office of a teacher (1 Corinthians 4:17); to impart instruction and instill doctrine (Acts 11:26)."[18] In a general sense, preaching and teaching are the same (Matthew 4:23, 9:35, 11:1; Luke 20:1). In a technical sense, preaching means declaring the Gospel, but teaching can also include declaring the Gospel.

On the one hand, *didaskein* means to teach the Gospel. But the word means more than that. It means to teach doctrine and different aspects of Christ's life.[19]

I like what Runia says:

> In the missionary preaching, the kerygma will be in the foreground. In the preaching to the congregation the emphasis will be on the unfolding of the message, showing all its implications for faith and life. But we should never forget that the Christian congregation too is constantly in need of hearing the kerygma.[20]

> As it pertains to today, pastors are encouraged to teach the "whole counsel of God."[21] Teaching is preaching and teaching. It is expository preaching. It is textual preaching. It is taking a passage and making

it applicable to a particular need in the congregation, whether it is on salvation or on how to deal with temptation.

Propheteuein

The word "prophet" has its origin in the Old Testament, where a man spoke the Word of God by revelation (Deuteronomy 18:18; Jeremiah 15:19; Amos 3:7). In the New Testament, a prophet is a gift and sometimes an office (1 Corinthians 12:28; Ephesians 4:11). The main function of the New Testament prophet is to edify, encourage, and console the congregation (1 Corinthians 14:3). Gerald Friedrick in *The Theological Dictionary of the New Testament* adds:

> The prophet is the Spirit-endowed counselor of the community who tells us what to do in a specific situation; who blames and praises, whose preaching contains admonition and comfort, the call for repentance and promise.[22]

Prophetic preaching today is preaching with authority and power. It is calling sin, sin. It is confronting people with the Word of God. It is urging people to make changes in their lives wherever necessary.[23] For today, prophesying—in the Old Testament sense of receiving new revelation that adds to the canon of Scripture—has ceased.

Parakalein

Parakalein, according to Otto Schmitz in *The Theological Dictionary of the New Testament*, has a threefold meaning in the New Testament:

It is used for people who come to Christ praying for help.

It is used for exhorting people from the Gospel.

It is used for eschatological consolation and comfort.[24]

Runia says:

. . . both *propheteuein* and *parakalein* teach us that true preaching is not recounting and unfolding the message about Jesus Christ in the abstract, but also requires that this message be applied to the concrete situation of the hearers. Christian preaching thus has a critical, a consoling and guiding function.[25]

Exhorting preaching, as it applies to pastoral preaching today, has the idea of coming alongside the members of the congregation and helping them—comforting, and consoling the church when the need exists (for example, at a death). The main idea is for the pastor to come alongside and to encourage and build up the faith of those under his care.[26]

In summary, the New Testament words defined in this section tell us how to preach. *Kerussein* says we should preach God's message joyfully—and emphasizes that we should preach God's Word authoritatively.

Euangelizesthai, a synonym of *kerussein*, emphasizes that the pastor has a joyful message to preach—the message of salvation. The pastor, then, should preach the Gospel joyfully, not with a sad face or in a somber or depressing mood. *Euangelizesthai* is evangelistic preaching. This word emphasizes that the pastor should preach evangelistic sermons. Paul advises the pastor to *do the work of an evangelist* (2 Timothy 4:5).

Didaskein emphasizes that pastoral preaching should have an aspect of teaching. In other words, a pastor's sermon should be didactic and instructional.

Propheteuein suggests that the pastor's sermon should sometimes be confrontational: *Whom we preach, warning every man* (Colossians 1:28).

Parakalein suggests that sometimes pastors need to be comforting in their preaching. Sometimes the pastor needs to come alongside of those in his congregation and to comfort them through his preaching. Sometimes he needs to be encouraging in his sermons. Most times a pastor needs to balance his sermons by talking about the grace and love of God, so that people do not go home only hearing confrontational and instructional sermons.

Let us now examine the goal of preaching.

Biblical preaching is goal-oriented.

The American Heritage Dictionary of the English Language (1995) describes a goal as, "the purpose toward which an endeavor is directed; an objective." Goal-oriented preaching is simply preaching with a goal in mind. I will further define this by answering two questions:

1. Why is it important to have a goal in preaching?

Whenever a pastor preaches with a goal in mind, he preaches more clearly. People understand what the preacher is saying, and therefore he is more effective.

A goal makes the difference between being a good preacher and an excellent preacher. Let me illustrate it this way: good preaching is like going on a planned holiday trip with all the right gear—a well-running car, money, proper medical insurance, and a happy family. Bad preaching is like getting into your car and driving around for a week without a destination—the best of church families will be frustrated in twenty minutes.

Establishing a goal in preaching gives the speaker a direction in which to aim his words. Having reached the goal, the preacher can then say, "I have accomplished my mission." A goal in preaching will allow the preacher to relax and will cause the congregation to relax. A goal in preaching will give unity of thought and progression.

2. What is the goal of preaching?

The first goal in preaching is to win the non-Christian to faith in Christ. This is done by preaching the Gospel. A preacher attains the conversion of non-Christians by preaching that one can be "born again" (John 3:5)—and that one's life can be transformed by believing that Jesus died and was resurrected for the sins of all mankind (John 1:9, 12). The goal is to create within an individual a belief in the Gospel, thereby causing the hearer to ask Christ to become Savior and Lord of his or her life.

The second goal is to help Christians mature in their faith. This is done by preaching sermons that help Christians to live a Spirit-filled life, to live a life separated from the world, and to motivate them to have a head-and-heart knowledge of the Scriptures. The *Theological Dictionary of the New Testament* describes mature as being whole, complete and in the total will of God.[27]

An example of the goal of preaching is found in Matthew 28:19-20 (KJV):

> *Go ye therefore, and teach all nations, baptizing them in the name of the Father, and of the Son, and of the Holy Ghost:*

Teaching them to observe all things whatsoever I have commanded you: and, lo, I am with you alway, even unto the end of the world. Amen.

This example emphasizes two commands found in the main verb "disciple." The first command is found in the words "disciple" and "baptize." Together these words emphasize a one-time experience and evangelism. As a crisis experience, "disciple" emphasizes a starting point in becoming a Christian. The term disciple (*mathetes*) is regularly used in the Gospel of Luke and the Book of Acts to designate the person who has placed his faith in Jesus Christ (Luke 6:13). In Acts 9:26, Paul was called a disciple. In Acts 14:21-22, Paul went to make disciples. Those who responded to the Gospel were called disciples.[28] The aorist tense used here emphasizes the beginning experience with existing results.

"Baptize" also emphasizes a one-time experience. People who respond to the Gospel are baptized.

The second command is found in the word "disciple" modified by the participle "teach." One not only becomes a disciple of Jesus Christ at a particular time, but the participle "teach" here emphasizes that we continue to be disciples of Jesus Christ by learning about Him every day of our lives. Peter is a good example of one who is a follower of Jesus Christ all his life, which is what the word "disciple" also means.

Teaching is a life-long process. We teach people the Word of God from week-to-week. We teach people to become disciples of Jesus Christ.

Christ's command, therefore, was not to declare the Gospel and then leave the converts alone to flounder in faith. His command was to declare the Gospel and then baptize and teach them. The apostle Paul clearly understood this when he wrote:

> *Whom we preach, warning every man, and teaching every man in all wisdom; that we may present every man perfect in Christ Jesus:*
> *Whereunto I also labour, striving according to his working, which worketh in me mightily.*
> *(Colossians 1:28-29, KJV)*

These verses teach that we should aim for something whenever we preach. Here Paul aims for the privilege of *presenting every man perfect in Christ* at the last day.[29] The main idea in these verses is that Paul preaches with the objective of presenting mature Christians to Jesus when He returns. This, of course, is done by preaching the Word of God.[30]

Now I want to center our attention on homiletical order.

Biblical preaching has homiletical order.

Since the time of Jesus, preaching has become a simple matter. Historically, a sermon has one *telos*—a main point, a proposition, or a purpose statement. A sermon must have some logical sense for the audience to follow what is being said. In other words, historically a sermon is from one text and has some type of homiletical order.

Dr. Jay Adams, Professor of preaching at Westminster Theological Seminary in California, states:

Each sermon has a general purpose, a *telic* dimension that involves a *telos* toward which, out of which and around which all of the sermon moves. The word *telos* means the goal, purpose, end or aim. The *telic* note should dominate the message. The *telos* determines the preaching portion. The *telos* of a sermon may be one of several such *sub-teloi* or may be one of several such *sub-teloi*. It should be the unifying factor in every sermon, without exception.[31]

Listen to Martin Luther's words about preaching and observe what he says about logic:

The preacher should be a logician and a rhetorician, that is, he must be able to teach and admonish. When he preaches touching an article, he must first distinguish it. Secondly, he must define, describe and show what it is. Thirdly, he must produce sentences out of scriptures. Therewith, to prove and strengthen it. Fourthly, he must adorn it with similitude, and lastly he must admonish and rouse up the lazy, earnestly reprove all the disobedient, all false doctrine, and authors thereof. Young divines ought to study Greek and Hebrew together, and discern their properties, natures and strengths.[32]

The logic I am speaking about is natural logic. Not the type of logic that comes from outside the text and is forced upon it, but logic that is derived *from* the text. It is logic found by discerning the Holy Spirit's purpose in a text and preaching it.

The point that needs to be emphasized is that the Christian sermon has to have some type of homiletical order to truly be considered a sermon.

Next in our discussion is the importance of relevancy.

Biblical preaching is relevant.

What is relevant preaching?

There are many answers to this question. Most of all, I believe that to be relevant, preachers should stick to the Bible text in speaking to people about their need for forgiveness from God. In my study of the great preachers of post-apostolic times through the present day, I have found that these were men who knew their culture well and could speak from the Bible and apply its messages to their culture. For example, Martin Luther collected sayings from the ordinary people and used them in his sermons. In fact, he knew his culture so well that today his translation of the Bible into German is a handbook for the German language.

The great preachers of the past and present were biblical preachers. They did not speak about the social issues of their day from a primarily social point of view. Instead, they usually spoke from one text or one portion of text in the Scriptures. They were mainly textual/ expository preachers. Two classic examples of this method are Origen's sermon on Matthew 17:15[33] and John Calvin's sermon on 2 Timothy 3:16-17.[34]

Relevant preaching teaches salvation by grace. For several hundred years the Church stopped preaching salvation by grace. The Dark Ages was a time of deception that saw the Church and those searching for salvation burdened with the message of salvation by works and salvation purchased with money or goods. It was Martin Luther who re-discovered and re-introduced salvation by grace. Indeed, salvation by grace was a major theme for many preachers of the past, such as Bernard of Clairvaux, Augustine, and John Wycliff. Most, if not all, of the great preachers of today preach salvation by grace.

The great preachers also spoke to the masses. Their sermons were not for the upper class alone but for all of humanity. Martyn Lloyd-Jones points out:

> Another characteristic of expository preaching is that it is not merely an exposition of a verse or passage, or a running commentary on it; what turns it into preaching is that it becomes a message and that it has distinct form and pattern. Furthermore, it must always be applied and its relevance shown to the contemporary situation.[35]

History teaches that great preaching is relevant preaching. Relevant preaching is preaching about a cause. The great preachers preached salvation by grace alone and were brave men who spoke against social ills—social ills directly related to faith and the Bible. John Wycliff preached against the Popes, idols, the doctrine of transubstantiation, confession to the priests, and the materialism of the Church.[36]

In summary, effective biblical preaching is similar to the proclamation in a synagogue service. The synagogue service contained textual exposition. Rabbis translated the text from the original language to the language spoken. They explained what it meant from the context. The text was expounded. They applied the text to the audience. Since Christian preaching has its origin in the synagogue service, Christian preaching should be textual/expository in nature. Jesus, the Apostles, and most great preachers have shown that textual/expository preaching is the best way to preach.

Effective biblical preaching should be in keeping with the New Testament words that describe it. These words not only tell us what preaching should be, they also tell us how it is done. The words suggest that preaching should be bold and that preachers should preach with authority. Preachers are ambassadors of Christ and should act as such. Preaching includes declaring the Gospel and teaching different facets of the Christian life. The preacher should be true to the Word of God and confront people with the claims of Christ and comfort and console the congregation when necessary.

Effective biblical preaching is usually from one portion of the Scriptures. It may be from a chapter, a portion of a chapter, a few verses, a verse or part of a verse.

Effective biblical preaching should have some type of homiletical order so that people can understand what is being said. The sermon should have one main point. It can be a proposition or a purpose statement.

Effective biblical preaching is relevant. It is applicable to people's needs, or it is made applicable to people's needs.

Effective biblical preaching must have a goal or a purpose in mind. In this regard, Jesus and the apostles taught that the preacher should have a clear purpose in preaching. The preacher should preach with the clear objective of winning the non-Christian to faith in Christ— and of helping to mature the Christian.

Now let's move forward and look at two contemporary models of preachers who utilize the textual/expository form of preaching: Dr. James M. Boice and Dr. Herbert H. Barber.

ENDNOTES

[1]John MacArthur, Jr., *Rediscovering Expository Preaching* (Word Publishing, 1992), p. 36.

[2]William Hendriksen, *New Testament Commentary: The Gospel of Luke*, (Baker Book House, 1981), p. 351.

[3]Yngve Brilith, *A Brief History of Preaching,* trans. by Karl E. Matterson, (Fortress Press, 1965), pp. 8-10.

[4]Hendriksen, *New Testament Commentary: The Gospel of Luke*, pp. 8-10.

[5]MacArthur, Jr., *Rediscovering Expository Preaching,* pp. 36-60; Jay E. Adams, *Sermon Analysis,* (Accent Books, 1986); Ralph G. Turnbull, *A History of Preaching,* Vol. III. (Baker Book House, 1976)

[6]Klaas Runia, "What is Preaching According to the New Testament?" *Tyndale Bulletin 29* (1978), p. 8.

[7]Craig A. Evan, "Preacher and Preaching: Some Lexical Observations." *Journal of the Evangelical Theological Society* 24/4 (December, 1981), p. 316.

[8]Runia, "What is Preaching According to the New Testament?" *Tyndale Bulletin 29,* p. 8.

[9]Ibid., p. 19.

[10]Ibid., p. 10.

[11]Ibid.

[12]Ibid., p. 9.

[13]Ibid., p. 19.

[14]Runia, "What is Preaching According to the New Testament?" *Tyndale Bulletin 29,* p. 10.

[15]Joseph Henry Thayer, *Thayer's Greek-English Lexicon of the New Testament,* p. 390.

[16]Runia, p. 12.

[17]Ibid., p. 19.

[18]Thayer, p. 144.

[19]Runia, p. 15.

[20]Ibid.

[21]Ibid., p. 20.

[22]Gehard Friedrick and Gerhard Kittle, eds. "Prophets" in *Theological Dictionary of the New Testament,* (hereafter referred to as *TDNT*), Vol. 6, pp. 781-862.

[23]Runia, p. 18.

[24]Otto Schmitz, "Paraklesis," *TDNT, Vol. 5,* pp. 781-862.

[25]Runia, p. 20.

[26]Schmitz, "Paraklesis," *TDNT, Vol. 5,* pp. 773-799.

[27]Friedrick, "Euangelizomai," *TDNT, Vol. 2,* pp. 707-737.

[28]M. J. Wilkins, *Dictionary of Jesus and the Gospels.* (Downers Grove: Intervarsity Press, 1992).

[29]Arthur G. Patzia, *National Biblical Commentary: Ephesians, Colossians, Philemon,* (Hendrickson Publishers, 1984), p. 44.

[30]John Peter Lange, *Lange's Commentary on the Holy Scriptures: Galatians and Colossians,* trans. by Philip Schaff. (Zondervan Publishing House, 1869), p. 36. Murray J. Harris, *Exegetical Guide to the Greek New Testament: Colossians and Philemon,* (Wm. B. Eerdmans Publishing Co., 1991), p. 72.

[31]Jay E. Adams *Pulpit Speech* (Philadelphia: Presbyterian and Reformed Pub. Co., 1974) p. 12.

[32]Edwin Charles Dargon, *A Brief History of Great Preaching, Vol. 1* (New York: Burt Franklin, 1968) p. 37.

[33]C. E. Fant Jr. and W. M. Pinson Jr. eds., *20 Centuries of Great Preaching: An Encyclopedia of Preaching, Vol. I* (Word Publishing, 1971), p. 29.

[34]Ibid., pp. 88-96.

[35]Martyn Lloyd-Jones, *Studies in the Sermon on the Mount, Volume II* (Wm. B. Eerdmans Publishing Company, 1959-60), p. vii; (quoted by) Fant and Pinson, *20 Centuries of Great Preaching, Volume XI*, pp. 272-273.

[36]Fant and Pinson, *20 Centuries of Great Preaching, Vol. I*, pp. 236-237.

** 2 **

Preaching Models: Barber and Boice

In this chapter, I will demonstrate to you how textual/expository preaching will help your ministry.

First, I will give you three reasons why a preacher should follow the examples of Dr. Herbert H. Barber and Dr. James M. Boice and preach textual/expository sermons. Then I will look at the background of these models, their churches, their ministries, and their preaching principles. I will also include other observations I have made.

Three reasons to preach like Dr. Barber and Dr. Boice.

1. The preaching style of Dr. Barber and Dr. Boice is biblical, not merely topical.

Topical preaching dwells on a particular text in the Bible, while textual/expository preaching seeks to translate, explain, and apply the truths of the text. In this sense, textual/expository preaching is similar to the synagogue service where the Word of God was translated, explained, and applied to the congregation. It is my assertion that Jesus and the Apostles followed the synagogue idea of translating, explaining, and applying the Old Testament to the everyday lives of the hearers. Preaching the Word of God was central to the New Testament services.

2. Dr. Barber and Dr. Boice follow the example of the great preachers of the past.

Earlier I pointed out that all of the great preachers including Origen, Augustine, Bernard of Clairvaux, John Wycliff, Martin Luther, John Calvin, Charles Spurgeon, and Martyn Lloyd-Jones did textual/ expository preaching.

We are often tempted to make decisions regarding sermon topics based on pragmatism, concern with cause and effect, or with needs and results rather than with ideas and theories. Yet when we look at the success of our contemporaries, we wonder what we are doing wrong.

Ralf G. Turnbull, an authority on the history of preaching, in his book, *A History of Preaching, Vol. III,* lists approximately twenty-five different types of preaching practiced in pulpits today. These types include topical, life-situation, psychological, dispensational, missionary, preaching geared toward a particular ethnic group, etc. Turnbull points out that these types of preaching are being done particularly in the Western world, however, they are not biblical preaching.[1] This may be a particular phase in history. There is no doubt that the twenty-five types of preaching Turnbull lists meet a need in society. At times it may be helpful to the congregation for the pastor to use some of the above types of preaching.

The wiser choice would be to make a decision based on overall history, not on a phenomenon or on one portion of history. For nineteen-hundred years great preachers have been telling us that textual/expository preaching is biblical preaching and is, therefore, the best way to preach. I encourage you to follow the examples of the great preachers.

3. The preaching of Dr. Barber and Dr. Boice has produced successful growth—growth in the New Testament sense of bearing fruit in the church.

Pastors are often pragmatic people. In a pragmatic sense, textual/expository preaching works.

Both Dr. Barber's and Dr. Boice's ministries have grown in the New Testament sense. In accordance with John 15:1-8, their ministries are fruit-bearing—conversion of non-Christians occurs. It is the Lord adding to the fold as in Acts 2:41—"the same day there were added unto them about three thousand souls"—and Acts 6:1—"the number of disciples was multiplied."

Dr. Herbert H. Barber came to Calvary Temple forty years ago when the church attendance was at seven hundred. Today it is more than three thousand, making Calvary Temple one of North America's one hundred largest churches.[2]

Dr. James M. Boice came to Tenth Presbyterian Church, a congregation of four hundred fifty people, twenty five years ago. Today the church has over twelve hundred people attending on Sundays.[3]

Both ministries have obviously been successful in the area of church growth. Textual/expository preaching produces growth.[4]

F. J. May alluded to classical Pentecostal preaching being directly related to church growth.[5] Dr. David Yonggi Cho, pastor of the world's largest church, says that he does textual/expository preaching during the week.[6] According to John N. Vaughan, at least a quarter of the world's largest churches and approximately twenty-five of the one hundred largest churches in North America utilize the textual/expository preaching method.[7]

Textual/expository preaching works; it produces growth.

Let me share some background information on Dr. Barber and Dr. Boice. This information will create a better understanding of these ministers and their ministries.

Background of the models.

Dr. Herbert H. Barber comes from a small farming community in Ontario.[8] By today's standards, his was a poor home—receiving an orange for Christmas was a luxury. Says he, "Money was scarce then."

Many of his relatives on the maternal side of his family were professional people. His grandfather was a pastor. His parents, though, were ordinary farm people and devoted Christians.

Four people influenced Herbert Barber's life in particular. His parents were people of integrity. They were hard-working, loyal to their friends, and met all their obligations. They loved God and were committed to their church. They were sincere and without subterfuge.

The third person who influenced Dr. Barber as a young man was his pastor, B. R. Morrison. Of him, Dr. Barber said, "[He] was a Godly man who had a great love for people."

The fourth person of influence in Dr. Barber's life was Dr. Purdie, a former teacher at Western Bible College. From Dr. Purdie he learned the importance of study and the balance between mind and spirit.

Dr. Barber lived through the Depression era and learned, like others, to live with little money. He also came to recognize the importance of hard work.

These influences formed the character of a giant of a man. They helped him in pioneer-type situations where he built churches with his own hands. His background gave him the administrative skills needed in a large setting. His upbringing made him a man of integrity.

He received his grade-school education in a small country school. He attended high-school in a small town and furthered his education on a scholarship at the University of Toronto, where he majored in English and History. After the university, Dr. Barber attended Western Bible College for one year. His studies were cut short by World War II.

Dr. Barber completed the rest of his theological studies by correspondence, receiving an honorary Doctor of Education degree from the Colorado Bible College and Seminary. After serving in the Canadian Navy for a year, he took a pastorate at a small church, where he has remained to this day.

In retrospect, Dr. Barber feels that his informal education was the most valuable. He reads extensively and gains insight by listening to and observing people.

Dr. Barber cites Drs. Paul Rees, G. C. Morgan, Clarence Macartney, Thomas DeWitte Talmage, and D. L. Moody with influencing his ministry.

Dr. James Montgomery Boice was born and raised in Philadelphia.[9] He attended the Tenth Presbyterian Church where Dr. Donald Grey Barnhouse was the pastor. His father and grandfather were medical doctors.

Three people influenced Dr. Boice. Dr. Boice's mother was a deeply devoted Christian woman who had a close relationship with her son. They spent much time talking together. This mutual devotion was instrumental in the development of his character.

Dr. Donald Grey Barnhouse, his pastor during his youth, often paid pastoral visits to the Boice's home. He took a personal interest in the young Boice. James Boice read many books written by Dr. Barnhouse, and these books certainly influenced his concept of Christian ministry.

Dr. Carl Henry influenced Dr. Boice's evangelical approach to America. Boice and Henry worked together editing the Christian magazine *Christianity Today*.

Dr. Boice received his education at a Christian high school in New York. He received a Bachelor of Arts degree in English from Harvard University, a Master's degree from the University of Princeton, and a Doctor of Theology degree from the University of Basel in Switzerland.[10]

Other observations.

Both Dr. Boice and Dr. Barber are evangelicals. They believe that people are sinful by nature and their only hope is accepting the provision of the Cross. I will discuss this in more detail in a later section.

Both men have a deep conviction that they have been called to preach. Their individual calling has often been tested by invitations to assume other important jobs in the Christian community. Dr. Barber was invited to become the president of various Bible colleges, head of the missions department of his organization, and General Superintendent of his organization. Dr. Boice was invited to become the president and professor of several seminaries but also declined the invitations.

Dr. Barber and Dr. Boice are both committed to the Lordship of Christ in their lives. Pride, egotism, and selfishness have no place in their lives. These are not worldly men seeking fame and fortune via the ministry. Neither of them is interested in position or money, nor do they preach merely for the benefits their office allows, such as status or power. Both men have felt a genuine call to the ministry.

Let's look at Dr. Barber's and Dr. Boice's individual churches and ministries.

The churches and ministries of Drs. Barber and Boice.

Dr. Herbert H. Barber is the pastor of the well-known Calvary Temple in Winnipeg, which is an affiliate of the Pentecostal Assemblies of Canada. He has held this position for over forty years. Calvary Temple is the largest Protestant church in Canada, over three thousand people strong. It is a conservative, middle-class church.

Although Calvary Temple is a Pentecostal church, its style of worship is conservative. Calvary Temple is a multicultural, multi-lingual, and multi-racial church.

33

Dr. Barber has full-time pastors working in the Filipino, Portuguese, Spanish, and Deaf ministries. Volunteers work with the West Indian and the Asian ministries. These congregations meet separately at most times, but they also meet together.[11]

Dr. Barber is personally responsible for starting several ethnic churches out of Calvary Temple, including an Italian church, a Spanish church, and a Native American church. Dr. Barber is also responsible for starting three English-speaking churches in Winnipeg. One of these is Charleswood Gospel Temple, with an attendance of over three hundred people.

Calvary Temple's summer camping program is an outreach for boys and girls up to the teen-age level. This program, which Dr. Barber started, is very close to his heart. The church has its own camping facilities. Every year hundreds of boys and girls enjoy a week of summer activities and many of these same boys and girls find Jesus as Savior and Lord during this time.

The music program at Calvary Temple is one of the finest in Canada. It began to blossom about ten years ago under the leadership of Professor Reuben Johnson, Ken Austin, and more recently, Dr. C. E. Thomas. Dr. Thomas was formerly the music director with the Billy Graham Evangelistic Association. The church has won many music awards. Calvary Temple has a fine pipe organ, a full orchestra, a children's choir, a youth choir, a television choir, a sanctuary choir and many special groups.

Calvary Temple has radio and television ministries that cover the Provinces of Manitoba and Saskatchewan. In the spring of 1993, the church started a national television ministry that covers all of Canada on the Vision Network, a multicultural and multireligious station in Canada.

Calvary Temple has a large missionary program. Its members give over three hundred-thousand dollars per year to foreign missions.

Dr. James Montgomery Boice has been the pastor of the Tenth Presbyterian Church for twenty-five years. The church is located in downtown Philadelphia, Pennsylvania and seats approximately 1,000 people. Although there are two Sunday morning services, if one does not arrive on time, it is difficult to get a good seat within view of the pulpit. The ages of those in the congregation range between 18 and 65.

Tenth Presbyterian Church is known for its excellent music. Robert Elmore, director of music at the church, is a nationally known composer and organist.

Rev. Marion Clark, Assistant Pastor of Tenth Presbyterian Church, says it is common practice to have classical music in their morning worship[12] This is certainly uncommon for evangelical churches.

Tenth Presbyterian Church is unique because it has developed its own Christian education program:

> . . . written and developed by Dr. Boice and a former missionary, Mrs. Elizabeth Landrop, among others. It is designed to teach basic Christian doctrines. The nuts and bolts of Christian belief are taught through the use of Bible stories, with each year's course built on the previous one. The adult Bible school offers a variety of elective courses—some exegetical, some historically oriented, others topically oriented but all firmly grounded in the Word of God.[13]

One of the great strengths of Tenth Presbyterian Church is its outreach program. This can be seen by the annual missionary convention where funds are raised for foreign missions. Tenth Presbyterian has an outreach program to international students where they befriend and help foreign students in practical ways and invite them to monthly dinners. There is also an outreach program to homosexuals, an outreach to singles, and a tutoring program for students living in the complexes.[14]

I was impressed by two things about Dr. Boice's ministry while reading his book, *Making God's Word Plain*. In his book, Dr. Boice gives his personal philosophy for the role of the leadership of the church. He lists six attributes of an effective leader:

1.) A high view of Scripture
2.) Preaches the whole counsel of God
3.) Under the Lordship of Christ
4.) Strong leadership skills
5.) A concern for missions
6.) Discernible love

Let me touch on some of these points.

Citing a survey taken from Western Reserve University, Dr. Boice shows that most clergymen in America do not believe in the inerrancy of the Scriptures.[15] He believes this is an error. Dr. Boice not only believes in the inerrancy of the Scriptures, he was also the chairperson of the International Council of Biblical Inerrancy.

In stating that pastors should be preaching the whole counsel of God, Dr. Boice means that they should preach expository sermons. This is done with a book-by-book study of the Bible. It includes reformation preaching, doctrinal preaching, and preaching the grace of God. It is a call to follow Jesus.

A leader should be under the Lordship of Christ, possessing a willingness to commit his or her life absolutely to Jesus as Lord.

By strong leadership, Dr. Boice means that the leaders of the church should be scripturally qualified to hold office, particularly the boards of elders and deacons. Dr. Boice cites 1 Timothy 3:1-7 and 1 Peter 5:1-4 for qualifications for elders. Regarding his own ministry, he further adds that while no deacon or elder would claim to measure up to all these qualifications, they do aspire to meet them.[16]

As a pastor, it is my personal belief that such high standards produce strong leadership, unity, and growth. Not to follow after these high standards would attract less than qualified and committed people to lead the church. The pastor is often frustrated and ineffective when unqualified people lead the church.

Dr. Boice urges the local church to have a strong missionary program. Early in his ministry at Tenth Presbyterian, Dr. Boice instilled the importance of missions support in his members hearts and minds. The church's missions offerings attest to their strong support.

Love should be a discernible characteristic of the local church and its leaders. The leaders and congregation are to be committed to love all and care for one another. In a large and lonely world, the local church must endeavor to meet the needs of individuals. Tenth Presbyterian meets the needs of its people by forming smaller groups. The groups meet under several banners; it may be the choir, a home Bible study or various other groups. Groups may also be divided by age levels, geographical areas, and personal interests.

Let's now move on and look at Dr. Barber's and Dr. Boice's preaching ministries.

The preaching ministries of Drs. Barber and Boice.

Some have argued that the seeker-friendly service should be of central importance. A seeker-friendly service is one in which the primary intent of the service is to help non-Christians come to faith in Christ without giving offense or dealing with possibly offensive or inflammatory topics. Others stress cell groups, proper administration, the knowledge of church growth principles and their proper use, prayer, or a host of other things. The preaching ministry is the center of the life and ministry of both Dr. Barber and Dr. Boice. Effective biblical preaching produces growth. Drs. Barber and Boice have proven this.

Both ministries concentrate on the systematic preaching of God's Word. The Word of God is expounded in every service: the mid-week service, the youth service, the special services, and certainly regular Sunday services. The main objective of each ministry is outreach and soul winning.

Though both ministries have all the trappings of a large church-camp ministry, radio ministry, television ministry, Christian education ministry, music ministry, single adult ministry, youth ministry, etc., the heart of each church's effectiveness is biblical textual exposition.

Both Dr. Barber and Dr. Boice understand the use of the media and use them effectively. Both men have radio programs; Dr. Barber is also on television. A church growth specialist may look at these ministries and conclude that their success results from the proper use of the media. That may be partly true. However, a church specialist may fail to see that it is their preaching that is the heart of their churches' growth. This is not to suggest that a pastor should not learn to use the media effectively, for it is certainly an asset. Most importantly, though, a pastor should learn to preach like Drs. Barber and Boice do. A pastor ought to see preaching as the heart and soul of their ministry. In Romans 10:14 and 17, Paul said:

> *How then shall they call on him in whom they have not believed? and how shall they believe in whom they have not heard? and* how shall they hear without a preacher?
> So then faith cometh by hearing, and hearing by the word of God. (Author's emphasis)

It is preaching that makes the difference in church growth. People are looking for good preaching, and if you provide good preaching, they will come to your church. People are dying to hear from God. Churches are dying for lack of good preaching. Dr. Barber and Dr. Boice are providing sound, biblical, textual/expository preaching and, as a result, their churches are growing.

Let's move on and look at the principles that make Dr. Barber and Dr. Boice successful preachers.

The preaching principles and practices of Drs. Barber and Boice.

First and foremost, we find that both of these men are committed to the inerrancy of the Scriptures. In an article about preaching, Dr. Barber states:

> The validation of preaching is that God has spoken, and He has called anointed men to share His message with the world. I can understand why those

39

who do not believe in an inspired Bible are reluctant to give themselves to preaching in the grand and glorious tradition of historic Christianity. If we do not have an inerrant Word from God to proclaim, then humility and decency should compel us to speak softly and apologetically. For who among us is qualified to "lift his voice as a trumpet" to command the consciences of other men if it is just to our insights?[17]

In a personal interview, Dr. Barber said that one must not only believe the Bible in an academic sense, but also possess the conviction that the Bible is God's Word. He insists that a pastor should love the Bible and believe in its message. Additionally, Dr. Barber feels that a firm belief in the inerrancy of the Scriptures is primary to being a good expositor.

Dr. Boice spoke at length about this subject when he was chairman of the International Council of Biblical Inerrancy. I referenced some of his remarks on the inerrancy of the Scriptures in the section about his preaching ministry. There is no doubt that he believes in the inerrancy of the Scriptures. He offers a bit of humor to illustrate his point:

> Nothing is sadder than the loss of this true authority, particularly when the preacher does not know it. The problem is seen in a report of a panel discussion involving a rabbi, a priest and a Protestant minister. The rabbi stood up and said, "I speak according to the law of Moses." The priest said, "I speak according to the tradition of the Church." But the minister said, "It seems to me . . . "[18]

Dr. Boice re-affirms his own view when he quotes Dr. Martyn Lloyd-Jones:

Lloyd-Jones is right in this analysis. The contemporary decline in (expository) preaching is due in large measure to a loss of belief in biblical authority and this loss is itself traceable to a departure from that high view of inspiration that includes inerrancy.[19]

Effective preaching and the belief in the inerrancy of the Scriptures go hand-in-hand.

Additionally, both Dr. Boice and Dr. Barber are committed to preparation and prayer.

The reason I've put preparation and prayer together is that they are the same thing—they belong together. Someone has said the Word alone will cause people to dry up; prayer alone will cause people to blow up; but Word-saturated prayer will cause people to grow up.

Both of these men view prayer as an important part in the preparation for preaching. It is intriguing to see the similarity in their prayer lives. Both pray in selecting a series of sermons, both pray while preparing their sermon during the week, both pray when they are finalizing an outline, both pray when they are stuck with their thoughts, both pray before they preach, both pray during their sermon, and both pray when they are calling the congregation to a decision for Christ. Their preparation and proclamation is literally saturated with prayer.

Let's look at the pastors' individual sermon preparation techniques.

Dr. Herbert H. Barber

Dr. Barber has three standards that guide him in long-term pulpit work:

1.) Dr. Barber seeks to preach the whole counsel of God from year-to-year, preaching all the major doctrines of the Scriptures, such as the Atonement, the Resurrection of Christ, and His Second Coming. He also preaches all of the major truths of the Scriptures, such as grace, walking in the Spirit, overcoming temptations, and steward-ship.

Dr. Barber feels that preaching the whole counsel of God from year to year is balanced preaching—a congregation needs a balanced diet. There are times when he may interrupt a series of sermons because he feels that a specific topic, such as stewardship, needs to be stressed on a particular Sunday.

2.) Dr. Barber preaches to the needs of his congregation. This does not mean that he jumps on every bandwagon that comes along, such as the prosperity gospel or inner healing or the multitude of other popular subjects. Instead, he preaches a balanced Gospel, just as a good parent prepares a balanced meal for the family. Dr. Barber suggests that a balanced Gospel includes preaching all the major facets and truths of Christianity; it is not preaching one's hobby horse or preaching all the time from denominational doctrine.

3.) Dr. Barber prepares by anticipating a series. He usually knows what he's going to preach from week-to-week. Much of his preaching consists of series of sermons that last a few months or a few weeks, depending on the text. He begins by reading widely about a particular area of study. In his general reading, he gleans information about his series and stores it in his mind (he has an amazing memory). Once he has done his study and thorough reading, he then chooses his text. His text is usually chosen more than a week ahead. This may vary, however, as some texts need more time than others.

For example, if he is going to preach on the minor prophets, he begins to anticipate the subject. He reads widely on the minor prophets. He reads other minister's sermons on the minor prophets and obtains ideas by how they deal with a sermon or subject, and how they form their sermons.

Dr. Barber has a basic routine for sermon preparation that he follows from week-to-week. On Monday, he selects his text, writes a simple outline, and does some brainstorming. During the week he uses his time as an incubation period to think about the sermon. In fact, without an incubation period he finds it difficult to preach. He feels an incubation period is necessary to be fresh and relevant. He feels the text must speak to him again, becoming alive to him again. During the week he may do some general reading on the subject, making a mental file. By Thursday or Friday he puts his sermon in some systematic order. He usually selects three areas of application. On Saturday, he writes his final draft, removing anything redundant. His written sermon is somewhere between a full script and an outline.

Dr. James M. Boice

Dr. Boice is also committed to preparing his sermons properly. Rev. Marion Clark, Assistant Pastor to Dr. Boice states:

> He usually spends three full days in preparing to speak on Sunday. He does his preparation at home on a computer, usually from the original languages. In addition, he does much reading to supplement his sermons.[20]

There are six things that Dr. Boice finds helpful in sermon preparation.[21]

1.) Dr. Boice sets aside and fiercely defends the necessary time for study. This is how his day is divided: the morning is devoted to study, the afternoon is given to administration and counseling, and the evening is given to light reading and visitation. During his holiday time, he reads heavy and technical works (books).[22] Early in his ministry he did not have many books, so he went once a week to a local seminary library. At the library, he did work on his texts for Sunday and explored other areas by means of the books that were there. Now he spends three days a week working at home. He usually spends "one day a week in general work on the texts, in commentaries and on other sermon-related readings. Then two additional days, organizing and (usually) writing each of the two sermons."[23]

2.) Dr. Boice blocks out the verses to be studied. He selects the verses in several ways: a thought in a verse, isolated statements (as in the Beatitudes), a paragraph by itself, or a story or part of a story (as in the life of Abraham). In the summer, he outlines his preaching schedule, outlines sermon texts for each Sunday, and formulates tentative sermon titles and a focal point for what he thinks the sermon should eventually say.

3.) Dr. Boice investigates what the text is actually saying: "To learn what the text says, means to learn what the original author was saying to those to whom he was writing."[24] He states that the preacher needs to study the context, the flow of thought, and the words of the text, especially verbs. He feels that:

> . . . the task of seeking to find out what the text actually says, and not merely what we want it to say, is the most important thing of all. Textual/expository preaching is preaching from a Bible text; it is preaching what God is saying in and through a text. Anything else is necessarily less than that, however true or relevant the other words may be.[25]

4.) Dr. Boice determines clearly the main parts or central teachings of the passage.

He feels that a sermon should have one main idea, and everything else is subordinate to that idea. But he points out that this is not always true.[26]

5.) Dr. Boice develops an outline that unfolds his main point or points.

Here are some suggestions:

> . . . develop an outline that effectively
> expresses the content of the text we are
> expounding. Sometimes, particularly in the
> didactic portions of the New Testament, the
> outline will practically leap out of the passage
> itself. At other times the development of an
> effective outline will be harder. It may be
> necessary to list several things the text does
> not say before highlighting the one thing it
> does, particularly if the misconceptions are
> likely to be in people's minds. An outline may
> express parallel statements of a simple idea.
> The Psalms generally use parallel constructions.
> An outline may follow the parallels. Some
> outlines may be unfolding points of a story.[27]

He says, "We should forget alliteration. We should
aim for clarity instead of cuteness."[28] He reminds us that
people are more interested in what God is saying to them
from a sermon, than in cuteness. Dr. Boice encourages
preachers to keep on working on outlines. In his earlier
ministry, he spent much time in outlining, but with time
and experience, it got easier.

6.) Dr. Boice develops clear applications. This
is a difficult part of preaching for him. He
suggests:

> . . . try for variety in this area, using
> different outlines and placing applications
> where they are not necessarily expected. Of
> course, most sermons need a strong appli-
> cation at the end as a conclusion.[29]

Having looked at Dr. Barber's and Dr. Boice's preparations, we will examine the third principle evident in both men's preaching ministry: their commitment to homiletical order.

What is homiletical order? When some people hear of homiletical order, they think of a complicated method of logic and argumentation. Others may think of a complicated method of communication, but that is not what trained homileticians use today. They see homiletics as a science that seeks to organize a sermon simply and logically. Dr. Barber's and Dr. Boice's preaching represents this school of thought. The logical order seen in their sermons is known as deductive logic. Deductive logic is where the main point or proposition is stated and explained. A few thoughts that are put together and given a title would be called a discourse, a talk, a speech—but not a sermon.

One may best understand this by looking at one of Dr. Boice's sermons. As outlined below, notice there are several parts to his sermon from John 1:15-18.

TOPIC: THE UNIQUE CHRIST.
TEXT: John 1:15-18.
INTRODUCTION.
PROPOSITION: In verses 15-18, John describes four things that make Jesus unique:

    I.) CHRIST IS UNIQUE IN HIS ORIGINS (Vs. 15).

    II.) CHRIST IS A UNIQUE CHANNEL OF GOD'S BLESSING (Vs. 16).

    III.) CHRIST IS THE UNIQUE SOURCE OF GRACE AND TRUTH (Vs. 17).

    IV.) CHRIST IS UNIQUE BECASUE HE IS THE ONLY ONE WHO HAS SEEN GOD (Vs. 18).
CONCLUSION AND APPLICATION.

Beginning the outline is a topic that draws attention to the subject. The topic is "The Unique Christ." Here, the subject is the divinity of Christ. Next is the text, John 1:15-18; the Scriptures from which the sermon is taken. Then follows the introduction. In the introduction, Dr. Boice states his proposition or main point. He wants to show the four things that make Christ unique, from verses 15-18. There is a question asked of the proposition: What are the four things that describe Jesus as unique in John 1:15-18?

There are four main points. Important to note here is that the points in the body of the sermon modify the proposition—four things that make Christ unique.

Finally, in his conclusion Dr. Boice summarizes his thoughts. He puts his application with his conclusion. This is a matter of choice, not of order. Remember, the conclusion ends the sermon.

The following is how Dr. Boice's sermon may appear in completion:

TOPIC: THE UNIQUE CHRIST[30]
TEXT: John 1:15-18
INTRODUCTION: In French, John 3:16 is translated: "For God so loved the world that he gave his unique son." Unique means being without a like or equal, single in kind or excellence, matchless.

PROPOSITION: In verses 15-18 John describes four things that make Jesus unique:

I.) CHRIST IS UNIQUE IN HIS ORIGINS: (Vs. 15): "He that cometh after me is preferred before me: for he was before me."

a.) Here it is talking about His existing before John the Baptist.

b.) He was one with the Father before He came to earth. Abraham saw Him in his day (John 8:56). Isaiah saw Him (Isaiah 6:1-3).

c.) The New Testament often refers to the pre-existent Christ (Hebrews 1:1-2 and Philippians 2:5-8).

d.) Jesus was not only a man, but also the Son of God, always existing.

II.) CHRIST IS UNIQUE AS A CHANNEL OF GOD'S BLESSING: (Vs. 16): "And of his fullness have all we received, and grace for grace."

a.) This is talking about common grace: everything truly good that comes into your life—health, prosperity, knowledge, friendship, good times, whatever it is comes from God. It is illustrated by the prophet and his harlot wife: a picture of God and us (Hosea 2:5, 8)

b.) All Christians are recipients of God's blessing through the person of our Lord Jesus Christ. He satisfies our thirst and hunger. He is the Bread of Life and He is the Water of Life.

Illustration: John Newton's poem and a Keswick hymn.

III.) CHRIST IS UNIQUE AS THE SOURCE OF GRACE AND TRUTH: (Vs. 17): *"but* grace and truth came by Jesus Christ."

a.) The contrast is between law and grace. The law failed to declare man righteous. In the New Testament, righteousness is based upon Christ and Christ's character.

IV.) CHRIST IS UNIQUE BECAUSE HE IS THE ONLY ONE IN WHOM WE SEE GOD: (Vs. 18): "No man hath seen God at any time; the only begotten Son, who is in the bosom of the Father, he hath declared him."

a.) The first part of the statement is universally accepted.

b.) Christ came in a way to make God known.

CONCLUSION AND APPLICATION:

a.) What is your reaction to these things?

b.) Do you know the truth of them personally?

c.) You can know these things by faith in Jesus Christ.

Observe from the above sermon how the sub-points modify and clarify the major points. Let me illustrate from the first main point of John 1:15-18: CHRIST IS UNIQUE IN HIS ORIGINS.

The main point is that Christ is unique in His origins; the sub-point shows how He is unique. He is unique because He pre-existed before creation. Dr. Boice's illustrations clarify the main point of the sermon. Here his illustrations are from the Scriptures that talk about the pre-existent Christ.

Let's take another example from his second major point: Christ is unique as a channel of God's blessings. The sub-point is about common grace. He illustrates common grace (God's unchanging love for all of us) by telling the story of Hosea and his love for his harlot wife.

Throughout this sermon he is applying the text, but in his conclusion he drives home his final point and makes his major application. Dr. Boice applies the text by asking two questions and making a statement: What is your reaction to these things? Do you know the truth of them personally? You can know these things by faith in Jesus Christ.

The logic used here comes from the text; it is not imposed from the outside. The way to find the main idea or proposition of a text is to find the Holy Spirit's purpose for writing the text. Once the Holy Spirit's purpose is found, so also is the purpose of the text. The wise thing to do is to organize one's thoughts around the main idea, and then it will be a logical sermon—a sermon whose logic is not imposed from the outside.

Now, look at one of Dr. Barber's outlines:

TOPIC: MIND-BOGGLING LOVE[31]
TEXT: John 3:16
INTRODUCTION.

    a.) Everyone's text.

    b.) Three key words are: *God, loved,* and *world*.

    c.) Proposition: *God, loved,* and *world* teach some valuable lessons. What are the lessons that the key words in John 3:16 teach us?

I.) GOD—HERE WE HAVE THE MIND-BOGGLING PERSON

What God?

    a.) Not the gods of various religions of the world.

    b.) The God who is capable of revealing Himself.

        1.) The God of the Bible.

        2.) The God with incommunicable and communicable attributes.

        3.) The God of absolute power, wisdom, justice, perfection, wholeness, and felicity.

II.) LOVED—HERE WE HAVE THE MIND-BOGGLING ACTION. GOD LOVED THE WORLD.

    a.) Different from the religions of the world.

    b.) Book of Hosea is an object lesson of His love.

III.) THE WORLD—HERE WE HAVE THE MIND-BOGGLING DIMENSION.

    a.) No limits to God's love.

    b.) No restrictions or conditions.

CONCLUSION.

a.) **God**—the wonder of the Person. Perfection of all His attributes.

b.) **Loved**—the wonder of the action.

c.) **The world**—everyone, needy.

Notice the position of the world "loved," in the middle, linking God and world.

Observe in Dr. Barber's outline how this sermon deals with the text. The outline is derived from it. He explains what the text means, applies, and illustrates it to the audience. That is not only simple and biblical, it is also great preaching.

Having looked at homiletical order, I would now like to discuss the fourth principle common to both pastors, and this is Dr. Barber's and Dr. Boice's commitment to textual/expository preaching.

It is difficult to discuss their commitment without repeating myself because in discussing their commitment to preparation and prayer, I also discussed at length their commitment to textual/expository preaching. Therefore, I will concentrate here on why I believe both men are textual/expository preachers and then discuss how they do this type of preaching.

Let me first answer the why. I have observed numerous things that have convinced me that Dr. Barber and Dr. Boice are textual/expository preachers. Outstanding among those things I have observed are the following:

1.) From a survey of many of their sermons, I am convinced that they are committed to textual/expository preaching.

2.) Both men follow the biblical and historical definition of preaching.

Dr. Boice works from the original text, and then translates it. Dr. Barber works most of the time from the English text. Both of them explain and apply the text to the congregation.

3.) Their sermon outlines included in this chapter and in Appendix J are evidence of their use of the textual/expository method of preaching.

4.) Both of these preachers have reputations as textual/expository preachers.

Dr. Boice is a well-known biblical expositor in the evangelical community in North America. One of his tapes was used by *Preaching Today*, a ministry of *Christianity Today*, to motivate preachers for expository preaching. Dr. Boice pastors Tenth Presbyterian Church, which has a distinguished pulpit and is known for textual/expository preaching. For Dr. Boice to become the pastor of Tenth Presbyterian Church he had to be a textual/expository preacher. Dr. Boice followed the renowned textual expositor, Donald Grey Barnhouse. As I pointed out earlier, Barnhouse was Boice's mentor. Dr. Boice's view of expository preaching is expressed in one of Barnhouse's favorite Scriptures and a favorite of pastors who preceded him:

> *For as the rain cometh down, and the snow from heaven, and returneth not thither, but watereth the earth, and maketh it bring forth and bud, that it may give seed to the sower, and bread to the eater:*

> *So shall my word be that goeth forth out of my*
> *mouth: it shall not return unto me void, but it shall*
> *accomplish that which I please, and it shall prosper*
> *in the thing whereto I sent it. (Isaiah 55:10-11, KJV)[32]*

Dr. Boice believes he is the answer to Barnhouse's prayer when the latter prayed:

> . . . and he asked that God would never allow a
> minister to stand in the Tenth Presbyterian Church
> pulpit who did not have complete confidence in the
> Bible as the authoritative and inerrant Word of God
> and who would not have as his specific and unalter-
> able purpose the task of expounding it faithfully and
> well to the people.[33]

Dr. Barber, though less well-known in the United States, is recognized as a textual expositor in Canada.

Dr. Boice and Dr. Barber's styles of textual/expository preaching involve the process of taking a text and applying it to a particular situation. Their expository preaching is also systematic.

Dr. Boice preaches through one book of the Bible at a time, or small portions of a text: one verse, a few verses, or an entire chapter.

Dr. Barber's method is a bit different; he doesn't always preach through a book in the Bible. Instead, he preaches selected portions of the Scriptures from a book in the Bible. He does not use a yearly plan with outlines for every week. Dr. Barber's series may last three months. In between his series, he may deal with other subjects, such as the end times. However, his sermons are always textual/expository in nature.

5.) Both pastors are committed to relevant preaching.

What is relevant preaching? Some people would have us believe that relevant preaching is solely need-centered preaching or preaching about contemporary issues such as AIDS, nuclear war, the church's response to the race problem, etc. Dr. Barber and Dr. Boice believe otherwise. There are a number of reasons why their preaching is relevant: it is biblical, clearly applied, results from reflective thinking, pastoral, positive, and natural. Let us look at each of these reasons in more detail.

Relevant preaching is biblical. Both pastors believe the Bible is inerrant and ageless and therefore applicable to every age and every situation. They believe the Bible to be the best handbook on psychology. Dr. Barber and Dr. Boice believe the Bible to have the answer to all our needs. Essentially, man's behavior has not changed over time, so the Bible's answers to the trials of life are always fresh, alive, and as relevant as if it was written yesterday. For example, a much touted contemporary problem in our society is the decline of the family. The Bible is a veritable manual on family life and relationships, proving its relevancy.

Dr. Barber's and Dr. Boice's sermons are relevant because they invest a great deal of time in reflective thinking. Reflective thinking is not only concerned with the facts of a sermon being presented, but it is also concerned with the way in which the sermon is presented. The sermon must be acceptable to the hearer. They endeavor to present their sermons lovingly, joyfully, enthusiastically, and in an interesting manner. Reflection is imperative for these men because they have been so long at the same pulpit and must still be contemporary and fresh. Reflection allows the truths of a passage to burn into their hearts again before they preach.

Dr. Barber and Dr. Boice are diligent in presenting sermons that are pastoral in nature and content. Their series are timely, appropriate, and their applications need-centered. The needs of their congregation are determined from their pastoral visits and counseling. These visits and counseling sessions provide the background for their preaching and application.

The application of both pastors' sermons are clear. For example, in Dr. Barber's sermon on John 3:16, he is addressing a great need in our society: a remedy to low self-value. He addresses this need by driving home the point that Christ loves us. He illustrates and reinforces that point repeatedly, and re-emphasizes God's love in his conclusion.

Dr. Boice will preach, illustrate, and apply the Holy Spirit's purpose in a passage. This is exactly how Dr. Boice applies his sermon from John 1:15-18. He illustrates his major points, and in his conclusion asks two rhetorical questions: "What is your reaction to these things?" "Do you know the truth of them personally?" He solicits an answer. He then interjects: "You can know these things by faith in Jesus Christ."

Both pastors maintain relevancy by remaining positive. This does not mean they are preaching a "prosperity gospel." Nor does it mean their preaching is filled with fear, judgment, hell-fire, and brimstone. Instead, their preaching is answering the concerns of our society in a positive manner. Again, let me draw your attention back to the previous sermon outlines. Dr. Boice's sermon on "The Unique Christ," from John 1:15-18, talks about the person and work of Christ. In this sermon, he offers hope in Christ. Dr. Barber's sermon on John 3:16 does not focus on the fear, anger, and frustration in today's society but rather offers hope and forgiveness.

Relevancy is guaranteed by the natural delivery style of each man. Though it is quite acceptable in some Christian circles for good preaching to include shouting and physical movements behind the pulpit, neither of these men adhere to that style. A sermon that is naturally delivered in a normal speaking voice is often more acceptable. Rev. Marion Clark, Assistant Pastor to Dr. Boice, says his manner of speech is the same in personal conversation as behind the pulpit. Though Dr. Barber is passionate in his speech and gestures frequently, he is quite natural. Great preachers do not copy someone else's speaking style; they are natural in the pulpit and comfortable with themselves.

6.) Dr. Barber and Dr. Boice are committed to Christocentric preaching.

There are two prominent views of Christocentric preaching. It is preaching that focuses on Jesus Christ, and preaching that focuses on the Cross or the Atonement. Dr. Barber writes:

> St. Paul considered that preaching was the God-ordained means for saving men . . . his theme was Christ, and his passion was the souls of men. . . . The right kind of preaching is Christ-centered, cross-centered, Spirit-quickened, soul-winning, self-effacing, biblically-based, timeless and authentic.[34]

To accurately define Christocentric preaching, we must ask: "Where is Christ in the sermon?" Let's look at Dr. Barber's sermon from John 3:16, referred to earlier. This sermon is not only about love but it is about God's love; it is about Calvary's love. Throughout this sermon Barber talks about Jesus. The difference in the love Barber talks about is that it refers to Jesus' love. Jesus loved us so much He died in our place for our sins. Christocentric preaching must always point to Jesus. In Christocentric preaching, Christ is always the focus. All the sermons I refer to in this book are Christocentric.[35]

7.) Dr. Barber and Dr. Boice are committed to the evangelical message.

The evangelical message is the good news of the Gospel. The evangelical message teaches that Jesus came into the world to die for sinners, and that through His death, we have forgiveness for our sins. Both Dr. Barber and Dr. Boice are strong evangelicals and are committed to preaching the message of salvation. They regularly invite people to receive Jesus Christ and make Him Lord of their lives. The Atonement is an important element in their sermons. Dr. Barber's sermon on John 3:16 is definitely evangelical in its emphasis as is Dr. Boice's sermon on "The Unique Christ" from John 1:15-18. The sermon should compel the people to put their faith in Christ.

8.) Dr. Barber and Dr. Boice are dedicated to their pastorates.

Today, it seems as if pastors are moving every few years. Dr. Barber's and Dr. Boice's commitment to remain at one church is refreshing. Both men have been invited to many different pastorates and positions in their denomination but have consistently refused to move. Both of them feel a deep conviction that God has called them to minister at their present pastorates. Both men are committed to remain in their present pastorates until death or until God leads them elsewhere.

The nature of their preaching permits them to stay at one pastorate for a lifetime. Since they preach textual/ expository sermons, by the time they preach through the whole Bible twice, a lifetime is completed. Topical preaching does not give you that privilege. In topical preaching, a preacher normally exhausts all the topics he knows and has to move after three to five years.

Another reason why these pastors feel a need to spend a lifetime in one congregation is that in a city it takes a lifetime to be known. Each time the pastors visit someone or take part in a funeral or a wedding, people are getting to know them and in the process they are building their ministry, one person at a time. Both men feel that longevity within a particular congregation fosters growth.

In summary, looking at these excellent preaching models has revealed many things:

We have learned the advantage of following the examples of Drs. Barber and Boice and preaching textual/ expository sermons. We have observed that there are many important similarities between these men, as well as some differences that show the adaptability and flexibility of the textual/expository method.

We have discovered that both pastors are strong evangelicals, both have a sense of a clear call to preach, and the Lordship of Christ is apparent in their lives.

Both men have taken small congregations and spurred significant growth through their preaching style.

Dr. Barber and Dr. Boice place their preaching ministry at the center of their church life and activity.

Finally, we have looked at the principles that make both pastors successful preachers. In the next chapter, I want to apply these principles we've discussed and offer some methods to develop a textual/expository preaching ministry.

ENDNOTES

[1] Ralph G. Turnbull, *A History of Preaching, Vol. III*, (Grand Rapids: Baker Book House, 1976) pp. 163-171.

[2] John N. Vaughan, Elmer Towns, David J. Siefert, *The Complete Book of Church Growth*, (Wheaton: Tyndale House Pub. Inc., 1985), p. 352.

[3] J. M. Boice. "Keeping on in Tough Times" in *A Proposed Book on Preaching,* (Philadelphia: Tenth Presbyterian Church, 1993), p. 3.

[4] Donald A. McGavin, *Understanding Church Growth,* revised ed. (Grand Rapids: Wm. B. Eerdmans Pub. Co., 1980); C. Peter Wagner, ed. *Church Growth: State of the Art,* (Wheaton: Tyndale House Pub. Inc., 1986); John N. Vaughan, *The World's 20 Largest Churches,* (Grand Rapids: Baker Book House, 1986); Samuel D. Faircloth, *Church Planting for Reproduction,* (Grand Rapids: Baker Book House, 1991); Ron Jensen and Jim Stevens, *Dynamics of Church Growth,* (Grand Rapids: Baker Book House, 1981); Eddie Gibbs, *I Believe in Church Growth,* (Grand Rapids: Wm. B. Eerdmans Pub. Co., 1981); George W. Peters, *A Theology of Church Growth,* (Grand Rapids: Zondervan Pub. House, 1981); Wm. Arn, ed. *The Pastor's Church Growth Handbook,* (Pasadena: Church Growth Press, 1979).

[5]Wagner, *Church Growth: State of the Art,* pp. 209-210.

[6]David Yonggi Cho, *Successful Home Cell Groups*, (North Brunswick, NJ: Bridge-Logos, 1981), p. 146.

[7]Vaughan, *The World's 20 Largest Churches*; John N. Vaughan, et al., *The Complete Book of Church Growth,* (Tyndale House Pub. Inc., 1985), p. 352.

[8]Interview with Dr. H. H. Barber, Calvary Temple, Canada. March 17, 1993.

[9]Interview with Dr. James Boice. Tenth Presbyterian Church, Philadelphia, Pennsylvania. May 14, 1993.

[10]J. M. Boice. "The Preacher and Scholarship" in *A Proposed Book on Preaching.* (Philadelphia: Tenth Presbyterian Church, 1993), pp. 3-4.

[11]Rev. James Barber, Interview by author, October 27, 1993, Calvary Temple, Winnipeg, Canada.

[12]James Montgomery Boice, ed. *Making God's Word Plain.* (Philadelphia: Tenth Presbyterian Church, 1979), pp. 8-9.

[13]Ibid., 9.

[14]Rev. Marion Clark, Assistant Pastor to Dr. Boice, Tenth Presbyterian Church, Philadelphia, Pennsylvania. Telephone interview with author, May 6, 1993.

[15]Boice, *Making God's Word Plain,* p. 106

[16]Ibid., 116-121.

[17]Rev. H. H. Barber. "The Lost Art of Preaching," *The Pentecostal Testimony,* October, 1992, pp. 24-25.

[18]J. M. Boice, *A Proposed Book on Preaching,* chapter on "The Preacher and God's Word," Tenth Presbyterian Church, Philadelphia, Pennsylvania, 1993, p. 4.

[19]Ibid., p. 5.

[20]Clark, telephone interview with author.

[21]Dr. James Boice. "Expository Preaching" in *A Proposed Book on Preaching,* 1993.

[22]Boice. "Preacher and Scholarship" in *A Proposed Book on Preaching*, 1993, p. 17.

[23]Boice. "Expository Preaching" in *A Proposed Book on Preaching*, p. 10.

[24]Ibid., p. 12.

[25]Ibid., p. 13.

[26]Ibid., p. 14.

[27]Ibid., p. 15.

[28]Ibid.

[29]Ibid., p. 17.

[30]J. M. Boice, *The Gospel of John, Vol. I*, (Grand Rapids: Zondervan Publishing House), pp. 116-122.

[31]Taken from Barber's preaching notes that were given to the author.

[32]Boice. "Expository Preaching" in *A Proposed Book on Preaching*, pp. 2-3.

[33]Ibid., p. 3.

[34]Barber, *The Pentecostal Testimony*, p. 25.

[35]Other examples are found in Appendix J. An Old Testament example is found in Barber's sermon from Numbers 35, "The Hiding Place." What makes his sermon different from a rabbi's preaching from the same passage? Is it that he preaches it in a Christian church and a rabbi would preach it in a synagogue? That is partly true. The main distinction, however, is that the Christian sermon points to Jesus. In the sermon, "The Hiding Place," the Christocentric part is to see and refer, as Barber did, to Jesus as our City of Refuge, to refer to Him as the One we can go to with our burdens.

3

Practical Implementation of the Principles of Textual/ Expository Preaching

In the first chapter, I showed you that textual/ expository preaching was not started in some homiletician's mind, but originated in the Scriptures with the prophets and was cemented under the ministries of Ezra and Nehemiah. It was accepted by Jesus and the early Church as the norm. Textual/expository preaching was further described as being a sermon from a portion of the Scriptures—a sermon that is logical, has a purpose statement, a thesis, a main point or a proposition, and is always relevant to the needs of the congregation.

In the second chapter, I presented as worthy examples two pastors who are presently preaching textual/ expository sermons in large growing churches. It was my intention to convince you that textual/expository preaching is the best way to preach by pointing out the fact that textual/expository preaching has worked throughout history for the great preachers and it is working still for Boice and Barber—and others. It is working for me, and I am sure it will work for you.

In this chapter, I will give some guidelines on how to start on a journey of textual/expository preaching. I will go behind the scenes and show how this type of preaching is developed. We will use charts, preaching calendars, and other helps to develop a series of sermons for months ahead.

If the first part of this book is academic, then this last chapter is practical. In this chapter, I will focus in-depth on the successful preaching principles of Boice and Barber and convert these principles into transferable ideas for your use. As stated in the previous chapter, I have observed eight preaching principles. Once again, they are:

1.) Belief in the inerrancy of the Scriptures
2.) Adequate preparation
3.) Specific preparation of textual/expository sermons
4.) Homiletical order
5.) Relevant textual sermons
6.) Christocentric sermons
7.) Evangelical preaching
8.) Pastoral longevity

1.) The inerrancy of the Scriptures.

As we have observed, usually the problem in churches is not that pastors cannot preach, but that they do not believe in the inerrancy of the Scriptures. They lack the foundation to be good preachers. That is why this question about the inerrancy of the Scriptures needs to be settled, especially by pastors who see the Bible only as a book of literature.

Believing in the inerrancy of the Scriptures obligates the believer to live in submission to the Word of God. It is imperative that the pastor live out the Word of God in his everyday life. In other words, a believer should so live that others can see the Word of God incarnate in his or her life. It is fine to believe in and talk about the Second Coming of Christ; it is quite another thing to live in such a way that you are prepared for the Second Coming of Christ. It is one thing to preach about prayer; it is quite another thing to be a person of prayer. It is one thing to believe in the sovereignty of God. It is quite another thing to live fearlessly because God is in control. When we live out the Word of God, our preaching becomes far more effective than just believing it. Believing by itself is passive and ineffective.

2.) *Adequate preparation for preaching.*

Preparation is vital to preaching well. In observing a number of my colleagues who spend less than five hours of preparation per sermon, I have noted that their ministries are foundering. Preparation is imperative. Excellent preaching is not a coincidence. Excellent pastoral preaching is not merely a result of academic excellence or the result of long hours of prayer. Academic excellence and prayer have their place in preparation, but they are no substitute for hard work and proper preparation. Excellent preaching is also not a result of occasional hard work—it takes hard work day-after-day and week-after-week.

There are five facets of proper sermon preparation that we will discuss: preaching through a calendar year, prayer, selecting a series, selecting the verses from which to preach, and blocking out the time for study.

a.) Preaching through a calendar year.[1]

Some pastors preach topical sermons from week-to-week. Some do very well in preparing topical sermons week-after-week. Many worry all week long, trying to find an appropriate subject about which to preach. Sometimes the topic is not chosen until Friday and the sermon is not finished until Sunday morning. Sometimes, sermon changes are taking place in the Sunday School hour before the morning worship.

At one time, I preached topical sermons every week; it was a difficult, frustrating, and taxing method of preaching. Then I discovered a simpler method. I now preach textual/expository sermons and the pressure and worry of choosing a topic for the next Sunday is completely lifted. I preach series of sermons mainly from books of the Bible. At times, I have preached series on the Parables, the Ten Commandments, and the Beatitudes.

Another way to preach through a year is to fill the preaching calendar with all the special days of the year, such as Christmas, Thanksgiving, Mother's Day, Father's Day, Easter, Remembrance Day, Palm Sunday, and New Year's Day. Doing this will provide at least nine pre-selected preaching topics. Next, I look for any special emphasis of my denomination that I need to preach at least once per year. In my case, I need to preach on the gifts of the Spirit, the Second Coming of Christ, and the baptism of the Holy Spirit. Here I have three other Sundays selected for me. Then I will look for any special emphasis of my church such as a missionary convention, revival meetings, etc. If I have two special emphases, I have two other Sundays already decided for me. Of course, all of these special emphasis sermons are preached textually. If I have one special speaker for the year, I have another Sunday decided for me. If I take a month of holidays, that is four more Sundays taken care of for me. Together, I have nineteen Sundays not to worry about in a given year of fifty-two Sundays.[2] During the rest of the Sundays, preaching though a book of the Bible will relieve the pressure and make you more effective in the pulpit.

b.) How to pray in preparation for preaching on Sunday.

Every pastor should have a regular time of prayer.[3] This prayer time should preferably be in the mornings before heading to the office. This is a time of personal devotions. It is a time for devotional reading of God's Word. It is a time to pour out one's soul to God in prayer. There should be a difference between the work and the walk; the work is the pastoral ministry, and the walk is the time of personal devotions where spiritual growth is sought through the regular reading of God's Word. The work is a time for the study and delivery of sermons, teaching, visiting, counseling, administration, and the host of other responsibilities that go along with the pastoral calling.

During personal prayer, time should be spent in worship, praise, and intercession for the needs of others: the congregation, missionaries, denominational leaders, and the government. A reasonable time for study and prayer is 45 minutes to an hour. This is time well-spent, giving one the extra advantage of gaining spiritual nourishment from the study and preparation of sermons.

Someone has said that textual/expository sermons are the most difficult and time-consuming of all the different types of sermons to prepare. If you are having difficulty preparing the textual/expository sermon, you will find that you will often be moved to stop the academic part of your preparation and go to prayer. You may be moved to pray as you seek to select the right series of sermons to preach or to select the right verses from which to preach. You may find yourself going to prayer because you don't understand the Holy Spirit's purpose in a passage or you don't understand what a text may be saying. You may be moved to prayer because your outline does not make sense or you need guidance to select the right illustration and the appropriate application. You may feel helpless, though you have prepared the best you can, realizing that unless the Holy Spirit anoints you, your sermon falls upon stony ground. You will be moved to pray for those in your congregation who need to receive the Word of God and apply it to their heart. You will be struck by fear and boldness simultaneously, realizing God is speaking through you.

The pastor's life is a life of constant prayer, not only for the daily 45 minutes but throughout the sermon preparation.

c.) How to select a series.[4]

Dr. Boice selects his series during the summer holidays. His series usually consists of preaching through a book of the Bible. His selection may be based on a book of the Bible which he has not preached through yet, or it may be from a book of the Bible he wants to repeat. His selection of a series of sermons is based upon the assumption that the Word of God is applicable to all men at all times.

Dr. Barber's selection of a sermon series is usually by the same method as Boice's except that his is a shorter series. Boice's series on a book of the Bible may last for a year or more, but Barber's series may only last a few weeks or a few months. Dr. Barber often steps back from a series of sermons to deliver a sermon on a particular subject that he feels his people need to hear, such as prayer or the Second Coming of Christ, after which he returns to his original series or begins another series from another book of the Bible. Thus, a pastor may choose to preach a shorter series, rather than a longer, more exhaustive one. The length of the series can vary from preacher to preacher.

I started a method of selecting sermons different from that of Boice and Barber a few years ago, when I heard what one of my colleagues was doing. He got his idea from Dr. John White, the noted psychiatrist and author. I was told that Dr. White develops his sermon series from his personal devotions during which he goes through a book of the Bible day-by-day, making personal notations. His thoughts from his devotions become the foundation upon which to build a series of sermons. I started writing down my thoughts and letting them guide the development of a sermon series, and it has worked very well for me. I later learned that Augustine also used this method of preaching, with some differences. Augustine preached from his devotions. He preached from how the Lord dealt with him, in the reading of the Scriptures.

I use Augustine's and Dr. White's method as a starting point. I usually have my daily devotions from a book of the Bible, writing down my thoughts on the few verses I meditated upon on folded sheets of typing paper and leaving them in my Bible. When I am finished having my devotions from a book of the Bible, I file these thoughts away by book order. Later, when I start a series, I have a starting point. I now have some thoughts to draw from and build my series on.

There are three questions a pastor must ask himself when choosing specific sermons in a series. The first question is: *Has God burned the truths of this text into my heart?* In that one question are buried a multitude of other questions. Have I allowed God to burn upon my heart the truth of the Scriptures I am reading and meditating upon? What does this passage teach? What does this passage mean? How does this passage apply to my life? Am I living out what this passage teaches? How can I better live out this passage? What is wrong with my life as it relates to this passage?

In one case, I was meditating upon a passage from Luke about servanthood for several weeks. It took a long time before God dealt with my heart about this subject. Once I preached that passage a year or so later, it was well-received because the truth of those Scriptures on servanthood had been made real to my heart. I am not always that fortunate to have the truths of the Scriptures made real and properly applied to my life. At other times it is a difficult task to work through the text.

The second question a pastor must ask when deciding on a series of sermons is: *Does this series meet a need in my congregation?* For example, if the need in the congregation is faith, a pastor must ask himself: Which book in the Bible talks about faith? Does preaching from Revelation make more sense than preaching a series from Joshua? Why or why not? The obvious answer is Joshua because Joshua talks about faith.

There is a third question a pastor must ask himself when deciding on a series of sermons: *Is now the appropriate time to preach this sermon?*

Appropriateness of a sermon is decided by the mood of the congregation, or the time and season of the year. If, for example, while preaching a series from Joshua, it comes up to the Christmas season (the seasons of the year greatly determine the need and mood of the congregation), the series on Joshua is set aside for a few weeks in December and something that has more to do with Christmas is preached.

Do not be so rigid in a series that you are tied to it. Once I was doing a series of sermons on the Ten Commandments and I felt unprepared to preach about adultery in a way that would be appropriate and helpful to the congregation. The congregation was also unprepared to deal with such a difficult subject. About two years later, when I was preaching from the Sermon on the Mount, I preached about adultery. This time the subject of adultery was appropriate, well-done, and well-received.

In choosing a series of sermons, it is helpful to outline the book of the Bible that is to be preached, to study it, to study other minister's outlines of the same book, and then to write down all of the subjects dealt with in that particular book with the appropriate Scripture passages. Classify these subjects by good, very good, and excellent sermons. This classification is based upon the three questions which the pastor should ask himself in choosing a series of sermons. Choose only those passages based upon the need of the congregation, the appropriateness to the congregation, and the Holy Spirit making the truths of a passage real to the heart of the preacher.[5]

d.) How to select the Scripture verses.[6]

Dr. Boice chooses verses from which to preach the same way that he chooses a book of the Bible from which to preach. Using Dr. Boice's method, the outline of the book and the flow of thought determine the verses from which to preach. A thought or a unit of thoughts can be preached. In the narrative passages of the Gospels, it would be appropriate to preach a narrative as narrative instead of trying to preach it as if it were from the Epistles or didactic. In dealing with a long story, such as the life of Paul, it would be appropriate to break up the story into major divisions. One sermon can be on his conversion; a second, his call to ministry; a third, his missionary journeys; and a fourth, his imprisonment. The Epistles are more packed and the treatment can be didactic, with the exact approach depending on the training and skill of the preacher. In Romans, for example, Dr. Boice preaches one unit at a time, one thought at a time, and sometimes one verse at a time (if there is a complete thought in a verse). Case in point, his sermon on Romans 11:35 entitled, "The All-Sufficient God," is based on one question from verse thirty-five: "Who has ever given to God, that God should repay him?"

Another method of deciding the verses from which to preach is to find the Holy Spirit's purpose in a passage and to preach it. Jay Adams, in his book, *Pulpit Speech,* makes the point repeatedly that the Holy Spirit has a *telic* or purpose in every passage. For example, how does one find the Holy Spirit's purpose for the parable of the

Prodigal Son (Luke 15:11-32)? Look at the context. The context talks about the love of God for the undeserving sinner, therefore the love of God is the purpose of the parable of the Prodigal Son.

e.) How to block out the time to study[7].

In order to become a great preacher, it is imperative for the pastor to block out a time of study every week. Great preaching is not only a result of experience, giving apt illustrations, having the ability to tell humorous stories, or leading a disciplined prayer life; it is also a result of hard work. There is no way around it. Both Dr. Boice and Dr. Barber still spend a minimum of 15 hours of study for each sermon, even after many years of pastoring.

As a rule, I set aside four mornings plus an extra afternoon for study every week. This has worked well for me. Of course, there are times when I need more time and I've taken it. This also does not include Saturday evenings, which I spend in revising and praying for the Sunday service.

Three days of study in preparation for Sunday or a minimum of 15 hours for each message would be beneficial. During study time it is important to have sufficient study material. If the pastor does not have home access to enough material, then he should follow Dr. Boice's example in utilizing a seminary library. Commentaries, technical works (such as lexicons), and works by other preachers on the same text should, if possible, be borrowed and brought home to study. General reading can also supplement the topic to be preached.

I still remember preaching on the passage in Joel 2:21-27 about the latter rain and God restoring what the locust had eaten. A supplementary reading on the locust helped me to understand what the passage was talking about, and in the process helped my message greatly.

3.) Specific preparation for textual/expository preaching.

Let me remind you that there is virtually no difference between textual and expository sermons. The main ingredient in preaching textual and expository sermons is that your sermon usually comes from one text.

a.) Translation.[8]

In translation, the preacher is trying to understand what the writer had in mind when he wrote the text. The best way is to work from the original languages. I know few preachers who always work from the original text as Dr. Boice does. If the preacher is knowledgeable in the original languages, he should continue using them and not be fearful or frustrated by the original text. I find this is easier with New Testament Greek than with Old Testament Hebrew, since most preaching is from the New Testament.

Utilize the tools taught in seminary or Bible school. The interlinear text is also helpful. In studying the original text, it is helpful to understand what the writer had in mind by noting verbs, the construction of sentences, the historical and biblical context, and by being aware of special sayings unique to that period, such as "in Christ," etc. A helpful book used by translators in understanding sayings is the *Greek/English Lexicon of The New Testament* by J. P. Low and E. A. Nida (eds.), published by the United Bible Societies.

Another good tool is the *26 Translations of The New Testament* published by Zondervan Publishing House. In reading a verse, a section, or a chapter, observe the different ways a word, a phrase, a sentence, and a verse are translated. Take note of a particular emphasis on a word, phrase, sentence, or verse, and emphasize what the original emphasizes. In English translations, it would be best to go along with a particular emphasis or consensus. This process will help you to determine the meaning of the original text.

b.) Exposition.[9]

Exposition is done by explaining the text. Explain the text by finding out what the text means in its historical setting. Explain what the Scripture meant to the audience to which it was written. Explain what it meant to the culture of that time. Find out what was being taught by a Scripture by trying to find out the principles that are being taught. Transfer those principles over to today's culture.

If a narrative teaches obedience, explain how obedience was taught then and what it means today. In books like Revelation, where the purpose of the book is teaching facts, an expositional preacher is to explain those facts.

For example, the story of the Prodigal Son teaches about the love of God for the undeserving. In exposition, the preacher needs to explain how the love of God is portrayed here. He would explain the rights of the older and the younger brother and how property was distributed in Bible times. The expositor would explain the customs of the times as they pertain to Jews being with pigs.

c.) *Application.*[10]

If textual/expository preaching fails, it is often in the area of application. A textual/expositor has only begun his work when he has done all of his linguistic work and understands what the passage is teaching. The work has only begun when the Holy Spirit's purpose for that passage is understood. Now the truths must be made alive and relevant to the audience.

Application comes easy for some people; for others it comes only with much hard work. Most preachers sink or swim according to their ability to make effective applications. A person who can apply the text well is viewed as an excellent expositor; a person who cannot apply the text well is viewed as a poor preacher. Application is going a step further than explanation. Application is linking those principles in the Scriptures to obedience and showing how we can be obedient today. In application, the preacher has to envision how the writer might talk about obedience today.

Continuing to use the story of the Prodigal Son, exposition is explaining the love of God for the undeserving prodigal; application is showing how God loves the undeserving sinner and backslider. Application here is showing that the love of God is constant and unchanging, as seen in the character of the father. The minor truths of the passage must also be applied. In the Prodigal Son, this would include the minor point that unlike the older brother, a Christian should welcome the backslider's return to fellowship.

But to make a minor truth the major point of the sermon is wrong. Do not apply the minor point of a sermon so strongly that people fail to see the major point of the sermon. Make sure the main application is about the main emphasis of the passage and not the minor emphasis. Good application is not merely using a passage as a springboard, it is emphasizing the Holy Spirit's purpose in the passage.

When the truth of a passage is made clear to the congregation, that is considered good preaching. Good application is always relevant preaching.

Sometimes in application, facts are applied rather than principles—facts such as the Second Coming of Christ. In preaching about the Second Coming of Christ, the application may be the believer's readiness for the Second Coming. The fact is that the believer must live in such a way that he is constantly prepared for the Second Coming.

Another way to apply a truth is to use illustrations. Illustrations are like windows to a house. It is helpful to tell current stories to illustrate how the text may be applied today. In application, illustrations should be applicable to both the Christian and non-Christian.

Observe how Dr. Boice applies his sermon on "The Unique Christ." He asks two questions, followed by a declaration: "What is your reaction to these things? Do you know the truth of them personally? You can know these things by faith in Jesus Christ." Notice his application is both pastoral and evangelistic.

4.) Homiletical order.[11]

How do you create homiletical order? How do you outline a sermon? How do you organize a sermon so that it makes sense to a congregation?

To understand homiletics one must understand logic. Logic is a method of reasoning. The type of logic usually used in preaching is called deductive logic. Deductive logic is stating a proposition or main point and seeking to explain it.

Logic must be derived from the Scriptures. The main and minor points must come from the Scriptures. The main point must not come from outside the text, nor be read into the text. To preach logically, one must preach the purpose of the passage. Jay E. Adam's book *Pulpit Speech* is an excellent primer in this area. Deductive logic usually answers interrogative questions such as: "What?," "Why?," "How?," "When?," etc.

When preaching a sermon, the preacher first chooses the Scripture. Next the preacher must choose his words carefully. What he wants to say must be able to be said in one sentence. This is called the main point, thesis, or proposition. A purpose statement may be less restrictive to the preacher than a proposition. In forming a proposition, the preacher is limited to the interrogative sentence. In a purpose statement there is no such limitation; the preacher is simply stating the purpose for preaching a sermon.

There are three reasons for preaching a sermon. The first reason is information; the aim being to acquaint or teach the congregation about a subject.

The second reason for preaching a sermon is to convince or persuade the congregation of the importance of a subject, or the benefit of adhering to a precept, or the truth of a tenet, etc. The third reason for preaching a sermon is to motivate or impel the congregation to take action.

Let's take the subject of tithing and use it as an example in the three different purpose statements for preaching, using Malachi 3:8-12.

If the aim is to inform the congregation about tithing, the purpose statement would be exactly that: I want to inform God's people about tithing. If the aim is to convince the congregation of tithing, the purpose statement would be: I want to convince God's people to start tithing. Lastly, if the aim is to motivate the congregation to start tithing immediately, the purpose statement would be: I want to motivate God's people to start tithing today.

Each purpose statement will give a different way to approach and treat the sermon. The last two statements are similar in that the preacher is aiming to convince the congregation to start tithing. However, the difference lies in that the last statement is seeking to motivate the congregation to begin tithing immediately. Motivating requires a certain amount of salesmanship, using facts and emotion to impel action.

To illustrate the development process of a sermon, let's look at an outline of Romans 5:1-10 as it begins to take shape. Early in the week the outline may look like this:

TOPIC: BENEFITS OF SALVATION
TEXT: Romans 5:1-11.
INTRODUCTION.
PURPOSE STATEMENT: I want to motivate God's people to turn their lives over to the Lord by showing them some benefits of salvation.

I.) PEACE OF GOD (Vs. 1).

II.) ACCESS INTO GOD'S GRACE (Vs. 2).

III.) REJOICE IN HOPE (Vs. 3).

IV.) THE LOVE OF GOD FLOODS OUR HEARTS (Vs. 5).

V.) SAVED FROM THE WRATH OF GOD (Vs. 9).
VI.) REJOICING IN GOD (Vs. 11).

The following is how the same outline appears on Friday:

TOPIC: BENEFITS OF SALVATION
TEXT: Romans 5:1-11.
INTRODUCTION.
PURPOSE STATEMENT: I want to motive people to turn their lives to the Lord by showing them some benefits of salvation.

I.) WE EXPERIENCE PEACE (Vs. 1).

II.) WE LIVE LIFE IN ACCESS TO GOD'S GRACE (Vs. 2).

III.) WE HAVE HOPE (Vs. 3).

IV.) WE BECOME MORE FILLED WITH GOD'S LOVE (Vs. 5).

V.) WE WILL BE SPARED FROM GOD'S COMING JUDGMENT (Vs. 9).

CONCLUSION.

This is how the final draft appears Saturday afternoon:

TOPIC: BENEFITS OF SALVATION.
TEXT: Romans 5:1-11.
INTRODUCTION: What is in it for me?
PURPOSE STATEMENT: I want to motivate people to turn their lives over to the Lord by showing them some benefits of being a Christian.

PROPOSITION: Paul in Romans 5:1-11 describes for us five benefits of being a Christian.

What are the five benefits of being a Christian that Paul describes for us in Romans 5:1-11?

I.) WE EXPERIENCE PEACE (Vs. 1)

    a.) What is peace?

    b.) Peace is peace toward God. It is justification by faith.

    c.) Peace is the peace of God, compare Philippians 4:7, 9.

    d.) Peace is Jesus.

    e.) Peace is peace amid life's disasters.

II.) WE LIVE LIFE IN ACCESS TO GOD'S GRACE (Vs. 2)

    a.) Grace is favor. It must be terrifying to feel you are not in God's favor.

    b.) We have access to God's favor even though we sin (1 John 1:8-9).

III.) WE HAVE HOPE (Vs. 3-4)

Before we found Christ we were hopeless.

Illustration: Hymn, "My hope is built on nothing less."

    a.) We have hope that God is working in and through our lives to change our character.

    b.) Our ultimate hope is that God will bring peace to our world.

IV.) WE BECOME MORE AND MORE FILLED WITH GOD'S LOVE (Vs. 5)

Illustration: Hymn, "O love that will not let me go."

    a.) This love is like a flood outside ourselves that takes us over (Titus 3:6).

    b.) It is agape love.

    c.) With that part of God's character in us we can love the unlovely.

V.) WE WILL BE SPARED FROM GOD'S COMING JUDGMENT UPON THIS WORLD (Vs. 9)

There is coming a day when God will judge this sinful world.

There is coming a day soon when the devil and his followers will stand before the white-throne of judgment.

CONCLUSION: To the believer, Paul mentions five benefits of being a Christian. Let us accept them and enjoy them.

To the non-Christian, you too can enjoy these benefits if you trust Christ.

This is how the logic of a sermon may appear:

TOPIC: BENEFITS OF SALVATION.
TEXT: Romans 5:1-11
INTRODUCTION.
PURPOSE STATEMENT: I want to motivate people to turn their lives over to the Lord by showing them some of the benefits of salvation.

What are the benefits of salvation?

(Points I-V modify the Purpose Statement on the benefits of salvation.)

I.) WE EXPERIENCE PEACE.
II.) WE LIVE LIFE IN ACCESS TO GOD'S GRACE.
III.) WE HAVE HOPE.
IV.) WE BECOME FILLED WITH GOD'S LOVE.
V.) WE ARE SPARED FROM JUDGMENT.
CONCLUSION.

The important thing in learning to outline a sermon is to keep working at it until you learn to do it well. When I was having difficulty in this area, I solicited my wife's and children's help. To make sure I was clear, I would go over my sermon outline with them on Saturday night. If they didn't understand what I had to say, I would change my outline. I am happy to report that I have grown in this area because I seldom require their assistance now.

5.) *Relevant textual sermons.*[12]

Though I have written at length already about the importance of relevancy in preaching, I believe it is important to add a few more thoughts.

In order to maintain relevance, the preacher must stay within his or her abilities. It is important that the speaker knows himself. God has given special gifts of ministry to those who are called, therefore to imitate another preacher's mannerisms or vocal style is a second rate presentation at best. The more comfortable the preacher is with himself, the more effectively he can minister.

In the early stages of learning textual/expository preaching, it is vital to make sure that the series meets the needs of the congregation. For example, before choosing a series, the preacher would want to ask: Is there a need for the series I am going to preach? Is there a need to preach this series now or later? Even in the midst of a series of sermons, it may be necessary to stop or change because it is not meeting the needs of the congregation.

Another way to maintain relevancy is to be with people, to observe their behavior, and listen to them. Read novels and books about today's changing culture. Listen to the news every day, or read the newspaper, or do both. Become involved in community, school, or civic events. Do not become a hermit. Incorporate what is seen and heard into the sermons.

Apply, apply, apply, illustrate, illustrate, illustrate—that's how to preach relevant sermons. Apply all the truths of a sermon, but most importantly, remember to apply and illustrate the main point. Choose illustrations carefully and prayerfully. Most of the time, people will remember an illustration showing how the text applied to their lives better than they will remember the sermon itself.

Praying throughout the preparation of a sermon will help to maintain relevancy. Prayer allows the Holy Spirit to impress the needs of the congregation upon the preacher's heart. Sometimes the preacher is granted the luxury of choosing a series that has to do with a subject he or she is deeply interested in and which also touches his people's apparent needs. At other times, it may be a series on a book of the Bible that covers another type of need: the need for information. The book of Revelation addresses the need for information. Relevancy is not an issue here. In preaching about issues, such as the end times, the subject itself becomes the relevant issue being dealt with. For example, in talking about heaven from the book of Revelation, heaven is relevant to all believers because they are going there and have loved ones that they would like to join.

Remember the Word of God is always relevant. It is the preacher's responsibility to choose from the Word what will meet the immediate needs of the people.

6.) Christocentric sermons.

A Christocentric sermon relates to Christ.[13]

For example, when preaching about tithing, one way to relate the sermon to Christ is to ask: Would Christ tithe? Did Jesus tithe? Of course, He would and did tithe. This is not to suggest that Jesus is the main point of tithing, but in application, tithing can be related to Christ. We tithe out of gratitude to Christ for saving us. Further, only by Christ's grace can sinful habits be broken and tithing in a proper spirit be made possible.

In preaching about love, it needs to be mentioned that Jesus is the greatest lover of all. He always loves. Let's look at Dr. Barber's sermon about the city of refuge.[14] The sermon became Christocentric when he showed Jesus to be like the city of refuge. It is important to remember that Christocentric preaching requires a relation to Christ.

7.) Evangelistic preaching.[15]

There is a two-fold purpose in preaching: to win non-Christians to faith in Christ and to help Christians mature in their faith.

These two purposes of preaching must always be kept in the back of the preacher's mind. This is most significant in the Sunday morning service since non-Christian visitors normally attend this service.

In studying the purpose of preaching and the methods of Dr. Boice and Dr. Barber, I am convinced that it is possible to do both types of preaching simultaneously. Both of these men suggest that we preach the Word of God to the congregation and the rest will take care of itself. Dr. Barber says he is evangelical in applying the passage to non-Christians who are searching for answers. Drs. Boice and Barber suggest that you cannot do Bible preaching without being evangelistic. The two are the same.

8.) Pastoral longevity.

There needs to be a change of attitude regarding moving from one pastorate to another every few years. Successful pastors are those who are prepared to stay and *are* staying at one church. Drs. Boice and Barber are good examples.

It is vital for the pastor to let the people know that he or she has a lifetime commitment to his pastorate. Once the people are assured of the commitment of the pastor, their trust is easily won.

It is absolutely necessary for the pastor to be transparent in all dealings. Evangelists come and go but the pastor is there to stay. Trust must be built one brick at a time.

Finally, preaching textual/expository sermons will assist the pastor in maintaining fresh relevancy and therefore insure longevity in the post.

Conclusion.

The world is still looking for great preachers and great preaching. The other day I was reading the book of Ezekiel. In Ezekiel 22:30 I read, *And I sought for a man among them, that should make up the hedge, and stand in the gap before me in the land, that I should not destroy it: but I found none* (KJV). I believe this passage can be applied to pastors.

I believe God is looking for preachers, great preachers, to take their assigned places. My challenge to you is to say yes to the Lord; yes, you want to fill the gap; yes, you want to become a great preacher; yes, you want to become a textual/expository preacher.

As it is with so many things, if you want something, you must be willing to pay the price. Michael Jordan is the world's greatest basketball player because he was willing to pay the price to become what he is today. In a similar way, God is looking for people with a firm commitment to the task of preaching. I challenge you to pay the price of diligent study, of personal discipline, of working through an outline, and of praying through a passage until you know the mind of the Holy Spirit, and then speak the message God has impressed upon you.

I am convinced that if this world is going to be saved, it is going to be saved through the preaching of men like

Augustine, John Knox, John Calvin, Charles Spurgeon, and Martyn Lloyd-Jones. Strive to become a preacher such as these.

Given the chance, textual/expository preaching can turn your preaching around 180 degrees. What I've shared with you is biblically correct.

Jesus and the apostles preached textual/expository sermons.

The great preachers of the past preached textual/ expository sermons as do the great preachers of the present.

Strong growth has occurred in the churches whose pastors preach textual/expository sermons. Dr. Barber's congregation, Calvary Temple in Winnipeg, Canada, and Dr. Boice's congregation, Tenth Presbyterian Church in Philadelphia, Pennsylvania, are two examples of such growth.

Apply these principles and practices that I have laid out for you. I am convinced they will change your ministry and your church.

ENDNOTES

[1]See Appendixes D and F on choosing a series; Martyn Lloyd-Jones, *Preaching and Preachers,* (Grand Rapids: Zondervan Pub. House, 1972), pp. 165-204; Andrew W. Blackwood, *Planning a Year's Pulpit Work,* (New York: Abingdon-Cokesbury Press, 1942).

[2]See Appendix E for an example of a yearly calendar.

[3] John MacArthur, *Rediscovering Expository Preaching,* pp. 63-84; Andrew W. Blackwood, *The Preparation of Sermons,* (New York: Abingdon-Cokesbury Press, 1948); John W. Stott, *Between*

Two Worlds, (Grand Rapids: Wm. B. Eerdmans Pub. Co., 1982), pp. 180-254.

[4]John A. Brodus, *On the Preparation and Delivery of Sermons,* Fourth edition, (New York: Harper and Row), pp. 257-261; Stott, *Between Two Worlds,* pp. 211-254; Haddon W. Robinson, *Biblical Preaching,* (Grand Rapids: Baker Book House, 1980), pp. 51-75.

[5]See Appendixes D and F on choosing a series, Appendix E on choosing a yearly calendar, Appendix I on choosing a monthly calendar.

[6]Robinson, *Biblical Preaching,* pp. 53-56.

[7]See Appendix G on choosing a weekly calendar; Stott, *Between Two Worlds,* pp. 180-205

[8]MacArthur, *Rediscovering Expository Preaching,* pp. 303-320

[9]Ibid., pp. 228-302.

[10]Jay Adams, *Truth Applied: Application in Preaching,* (Grand Rapids, Zondervan Pub. House, 1990); Brodus, *On the Preparation and Delivery of Sermons,* pp. 165-170.

[11]See Appendix H on outlining a sermon; Adams, *Pulpit Speech* (Philadelphia: Presbyterian and Reformed Pub. Co., 1974); Merrill F. Unger, *Principles of Expository Preaching.* (Grand Rapids: Zondervan Pub. House, 1978), pp. 85-110; Jay E. Adams, *Preaching with Purpose,* (Grand Rapids: Zondervan Pub. House, 1982).

[12]Pierre Ch. Marcel, *The Relevance of Preaching,* trans. Rob Roy McGregor, (Grand Rapids: Baker Book House, 1963); Lloyd-Jones, *Preaching and Preachers,* pp. 121-142; Robinson, *Biblical Preaching,* pp. 191-209.

[13]Edmund P. Clowney, *Preaching and Biblical Theology,* (Grand Rapids: Wm. B. Eerdman's Pub. Co., 1961); Adams, *Preaching with Purpose,* pp. 146-152.

[14]See Appendix J.

[15]Lloyd-Jones, *Preaching and Preachers,* pp. 265-284; Adams, *Preaching with Purpose,* pp. 70-77; Lloyd M. Perry, *Biblical Preaching for Today's World,* (Chicago: Moody Press, 1973), pp. 151-171.

Appendix A

Pastors' Training for Preaching: A Survey

This preaching survey included twenty-four pastors from a variety of backgrounds, including Roman Catholic and Protestant groups, Evangelical and Non-evangelical groups, rural and urban churches.

The following are the results of the survey done by telephone. Listed are some of the questions asked and other significant information.

1. Training

a.) How many years of formal post-high-school education have you completed?

Most pastors had five and a half years of post-high-school training.

b.) What type of formal education do you have?

43% had University and Seminary training

35% had University training alone.

What this reflects is that while most pastors (78%) have had some type of higher education, less than half have had the advantage of a seminary education.

c.) Has some of your education focused on preparing you for the pastoral ministry?

100% felt that their training prepared them for ministry.

91% were generally satisfied with the training they received; and 4% felt that it was well above average.

54% felt their training was above average,

4% felt their education was below average

d.) How many courses in preaching (including public speaking) have you taken?

The average number of courses taken was two and a half. Most pastors were dissatisfied with the training they received specifically in preaching.

e.) Which of the following courses did you take in preaching? Please indicate the value of the courses.

63% took exegesis and felt that it was helpful.

57% took some type of homiletical theology.

55% did some type of practice preaching during their course work.

Out of the 24 pastors surveyed, only 3 took courses beyond the minimum required: 1 took communication as a preacher, 1 took sermon preparation; the third received supervision in preaching during an internship program. All three felt their course work was valuable training.

Only 1 person had an advanced degree in preaching (Master of Theology).

f.) Indicate the value of the following aids to preaching since graduation:

- listening to good preaching - 73%

- Writing out your sermon in long-hand - 62%

- The least helpful was listening to television preachers.

g.) What criteria do you use to evaluate your preaching ability?

Most pastors use two indicators to evaluate their preaching ability: 70% use the verbal responses of listeners; 68% use the behavioral responses of others.

The least helpful evaluation was an invitation to speak elsewhere (68%).

It is also significant that 50% used some type of an on-going evaluation, such as conducting surveys or seeking the opinion of worship committees, to evaluate their preaching.

2. The Act of Preaching

a.) How long do you spend in prayer and preparation for your Sunday sermon?

On the average pastors spent 3 hours in prayer and preparation for their preaching on Sunday.

b.) Do you have a purpose statement or proposition for each sermon?

95% usually have a purpose statement or proposition for each sermon.

64% prepare and preach with the non-Christians in mind.

81% prepare and preach with the Christians in mind.

c.) Do you have an outline for each sermon?

100% have an outline for each sermon.

d.) Do you use full notes or part notes?

70% use full notes most times; 12% do not use notes.

e.) Do you do biblical exegesis for each sermon?

82% do biblical exegesis for each sermon.

f.) Do you use helps in sermon preparation?

89% use helps in preparation for their sermons: translations, commentaries, etc.

g.) From where do you obtain most of your illustrations?

83% obtain illustrations from books; 70% from life.

Most pastors said that a good illustration is something that brings clarity to the sermon or illustrates a point. Most pastors select an illustration via a file system. Though most pastors agreed that they give good illustrations, others said they struggle finding them.

The general consensus has been that looking outside themselves, observing life, reading, listening and staying in touch with people, has been the biggest help in illustrating a point.

h.) How much time do you spend in study for a sermon?

58% of the pastors spend 6 - 10 hours of preparation per sermon; 16% spend 5 hours of preparation per sermon. Only 1 person spends more than 21 hours of preparation per sermon, this being the pastor with a Th.M. in preaching.

i.) What type of sermon do you most often preach?

74% preach textual/expository sermons; 24% preach topical sermons; and others preach psychological and character studies.

j.) Indicate the value of the following to pastoral preaching:

Pastoral preaching should be biblical - 98%

Preaching should be directed toward Christians - 98%

Pastoral preaching should be directed toward non-Christians - 80%

Pastoral preaching should be applicable to the congregation - 80%

Pastoral preaching has Holy Spirit anointing, a feeling that God is speaking through the minister - 99%

Pastoral preaching is appropriate - 96%

Pastoral preaching moves the audience to a particular direction/action - 95%

Pastoral preaching is helpful - 92%

It is motivational - 93%

Pastoral preaching is constructive - 81%

k.) What is good delivery?

1.) Many said, "It is clarity." Others said, "It is being understood, motivating others to change, having the whole person involved in delivery."

2.) 97% believe that good delivery is anointed preaching; 94% indicated that it is helpful preaching; 71% believe that we should use partial notes; 55% indicated that it should have a 30 minute limit; 54% preferred a 20 minute limit. More than 50% feel that a sermon should be between 20 - 30 minutes. One suggestion was that the morning preaching should be 20 minutes and the evening preaching 40 minutes long.

3. Needs
a.) 83% felt the need to develop their preaching.

The following are some of the areas in which pastors felt the need to develop their preaching: 61% felt the need to develop their public speaking; 49%, outlining; 50%, introduction; 58%, conclusion; 55%, understanding the passage; 61%, obtaining illustrations; 65%, making the text applicable to the audience; 55%, preaching the Gospel in the morning service, 55%, preaching more biblically.

b.) 78% determined their adequacy of preaching by their own feelings or their wife's feelings.

Conclusion
We have made four observations about these pastors and their preaching:

1.) Most of them felt poorly prepared for the task of preaching.

They felt that the courses offered to them at school were insufficient. In one case, a pastor who was taught at a good seminary and is now a Ph.D. candidate at Oxford University has never taken a course in preaching. A few pastors are trying to correct this problem by listening to good preaching and by having groups of laymen from their churches give them assistance and guidance in preaching.

2.) Most pastors were open to development in preaching, and we feel that if they are open, sooner or later something will work out for their betterment.

3.) Pastors pointed out two areas of great need: Outlining the passage and understanding and applying the text.

They needed help in all facets of outlining a sermon: purpose statement, introduction, body, illustration, and conclusion.

4.) Those pastors who spent less than five hours in preparation for their sermon had ministries that were foundering.

Appendix B

Survey Indicating the Results of Two Pastors' Preaching Seminars

I conducted two preaching seminars for pastors. Immediately after the seminars, I surveyed participants about the seminar, asking them if they had received any help from my preaching seminar. They gave me a score of four out of five; in other words, they gave the seminar a score of 80%.

Six weeks later, I surveyed participating pastors again to find out the areas where they were helped. The following were the questions and answers:

1.) Have you been helped in preparing a yearly, monthly, and weekly preaching calendar?
67% said, "Yes."

2.) Have you been helped in preparing to preach on Sunday?
71% said, "Yes."

3.) Have you been helped in outlining a sermon?
65% said, "Yes."

4.) *Did the seminar help to improve your delivery?*
64% felt improvement in their delivery.

5.) *Did the seminar help improve your confidence in preaching?*
80% felt the seminar improved their performance.

6.) *Did your attitude toward preaching improve?*
86% saw an improvement in their attitude.

7.) *Did your congregation respond better to your preaching after the seminar?*
68% felt immediate improvement; 73% felt improvement after six weeks.

Appendix C

Pastors' Theological Training in Preaching

SCHOOL	PROGRAM	PREACHING COURSES REQUIRED FOR GRADUATION
BETHEL THEOLOGICAL SEMINARY	M.DIV.	PRACTICUM A & B
DALLAS THEOLOGICAL SEMINARY	Th.M.	EXPOSITORY PREACHING 1, 2, 3 (= 7 HRS)
MOODY BIBLE INSTITUTE	B.A./ DIPLOMA	SPEECH COMMUNICATION
SASKATOON THEOL. UNION	M.DIV./B.TH .	HOMILETICS
WINKLER THEOLOGICAL SEMINARY	DIPLOMA	SPEECH COMMUNICATION

SCHOOL	PROGRAM	PREACHING COURSES REQUIRED FOR GRADUATION
MENNONITE BRETHREN BIBLICAL SEMINARY	M.DIV.	PREACHING (= 2 HRS)
ONTARIO THEOLOGICAL SEMINARY	M.DIV.	PREACHING PRACTICUM
TORONTO BAPTIST SEMINARY & BIBLE COLLEGE	M.DIV.	HOMILETICS (= 4 HRS)
WESTMINSTER THEOLOGICAL SEMINARY	M. DIV.	SERMON EVALUATION SERMON ANALYSIS SERMON DELIVERY (=3 HRS)
ASHLAND THEOLOGICAL SEMINARY	M. DIV.	NO REQUIREMENTS
CANADIAN NAZARENE COLLEGE	B.A./ B.TH	NO REQUIREMENTS
WESTERN CONSERVATIVE SEMINARY	M.DIV. (PASTORAL)	BASIC SERMON DEVELOPMENT " "
PROVIDENCE COLLEGE	B.A.	COMMUNICATION THEORY
CENTRAL COLLEGE	DIPLOMA	HOMILETICS PREACHING 2 & 3 (= 3 HRS)

Appendix D

Acts: Sermons and Public Discourse

SCRIPTURE	OCCASION	PURPOSE	AUDIENCE	COMMENTS
2:1-41 (14-36)	Day of Pentecost	points people to Christ	God fearing Jews	uses OT & NT Scripture
3:1-26	Peter heals a crippled beggar	points men to Jesus	Jews	but uses the occasion to preach Jesus. Scripture
4:8-12	Apostles before the High Priest for preaching Jesus.	defense	Jewish leaders	v.12. Jesus is the only name to be saved by.
5:27-42	Apostles before the Sanhedrin	defense	Jews	brings up Jesus' death
6:8-7:59	Stephen's defense before the Sanhedrin	defense	Jewish leaders	not afraid of of death; explained salvation
8:26-40	Philip preaches to an Ethiopian	points him to Jesus	Gentiles	explained Isaiah; God directed
10:1-47	Peter preaches at Cornelius' house	points people to Christ	Gentiles	God directed
13:16-41	Paul at Antioch in Pisidia	points people to Christ	Jews & Gentiles	salvation preached

SCRIPTURE	OCCASION	PURPOSE	AUDIENCE	COMMENTS
15:22-35	letter to existing churches at Antioch, Syria, and Cilicia	encourages believers to serve God	Gentile Christians	letter and prophets encourage God's People
17:16-34	Paul speaking to Greek philosophers	points people to Jesus	Greek philosophers	no use of Scripture—starts with philosophy (where they're at); works in the principles of Scripture
20:13-37	Paul's farewell to the church at Ephesus	encouragement and final instruction	church elders	similar to 1 Peter 5:7; not a sermon but similar
21:37-22:29	Paul speaks to a crowd-Jerusalem	defense (gives his testimony)	Jews	gives his testimony in defense
22:30-23:11	Paul before the Sanhedrin	defense	Jewish leaders	defends himself, he splits the group
24:1-27	Paul's defense before Felix	defense—preaches Jesus as the way of salvation	non-Christians	it seems Felix wants to hear Paul talk about salvation
26:1-32	Paul before Agrippa	seeks to present the gospel	non-Christians	v.1. defense yet v.28-29 seeks to bring him to Christ
28:17-31	Paul Preaches in Rome under guard	explains the way of salvation	Jewish leaders	presents salvation through Jesus Christ

Appendix E
Yearly Preaching Calendar
(1996 as a Sample)

7 **January**
14 Martin Luther King Day (15)
21
28
4 **February**
11 Valentine's Day (14)
18 Ash Wednesday (21) President's Day (19)
25 Lent
3 **March**
10 Commonwealth Day (11-Canada)
17
24
31 Palm Sunday
7 **April** - Easter Sunday
14
21
28
5 **May**
12 - Mother's Day
19
26 Day of Pentecost - Memorial Day Weekend (27-USA) - Victoria Day (27-Canada)

2 June
9
16 Father's Day
23
30 Canada Day (1)
7 July - Independence Day (4 - USA)
14
21
28
4 August
11
18
25
1 September - Labor Day Weekend - (2-USA)
8
15
22
29
6 October
13 Canadian Thanksgiving - Columbus Day (14-USA)
20
27
3 November
10 Veteran's Day (11-USA) - Remembrance Day (11-Canada)
17
24 Thanksgiving Day (28)
1 December - First Sunday in Advent
8
15
22 Christmas Day (25) Boxing Day (26 - Canada)
29 New Year's Eve (31) New Year's Day (1)

Appendix F

Choosing a Series:

The Gospel of Luke

Excellent

1.) Jesus' victory over temptations - temptation. (Luke 4:1-15)

V. good

2.) Jesus chooses disciples - types of people he wants to make winners. (5:1-11, 27-32)

V. good

3.) Healing of the man with palsy - healing. (5:18-26)

V. good

4.) Jesus heals the centurion's son - all receive help from Christ. (7:1-10)

good

5.) Jesus heals the widow's son - Jesus helps widows. (7:11-18)

Excellent

6.) Jesus accepts perfume from sinner - forgiveness. (7:36-50)

Excellent

7.) Jesus stills the storm - Jesus stills storms yet today. (8:22-25)

8.) Jesus delivers a demon-possessed man - demon possession. (8: 26-40)

Excellent

9.) Jesus heals the woman with a blood disease - Christ's power. (8: 43-56)

Excellent

10.) Jesus feeds 5,000 - Jesus is Bread. (9:11-27)

Excellent

11.) The transfiguration - prayer transfigures. (9:28-36)

103

V. Good

12.) Jesus has come to give life - whole life.
(9:55-56)

Good

13.) The parable of the Good Samaritan - Jesus forgives.
(10:30-37)

Excellent

14.) Sitting at Jesus' feet - Mary and Martha.
(10:38-42)

Excellent

15.) Consider the lilies - trust God, don't worry.
(12:22-34)

Excellent

16.) The Second Coming of Christ - being ready.
(12:36-40)

Excellent

17.) The Second Coming of Christ - watching.
(12:41-53)

Excellent

18.) Woman with the spirit of infirmity - need-centered.
(13:11-17)

V. Good

19.) How to get along in life - let God exalt you.
(14:11)

Excellent

20.) Invitation to the Great Supper - invitation to salvation. (14:12-24)

Sermons I Chose from Luke:

1.) Jesus overcomes temptations - temptation
(Luke 4:1-15)

2.) Jesus chooses disciples - losers make winners
(5:1-11)

3.) Jesus accepts perfume from sinner - forgiveness
(7:36-50)

4.) Jesus stills the storm - Jesus stills storms yet today
(8:22-35)

5.) Jesus heals demon-possessed person - demon possession (8:26-40)

6.) Jesus heals the woman with the issue of blood - Christ's power (8:43-56)

7.) Jesus feeds 5,000 - Jesus is Bread (9:11-17)

8.) The transfiguration - prayer transfigures
(9:28-36)

9.) Jesus has come to give life - whole life
     (9:55-56)
10.) Consider the lilies - don't worry, trust God
     (12:22-34)
11.) The Second Coming of Christ - being ready
     (12:36-40)
12.) The Second Coming of Christ - watching
     (12:49-53)
13.) The woman with the issue of blood - need-centered
     (13:11-17)
14.) Invitation to the Great Supper - invitation to salvation
     (14:12-24)
15.) The Prodigal Son - forgiveness   (15:11-32)
16.) A blind man receives sight - compassion
     (18:35-43)
17.) Zaccheus receives visit - kindness   (19:1-18)
18.) Thankful leper - praise guarantees wholeness
     (17:11-19)
19.) Lessons from children - childlikeness
     (18:15-17)
20.) The publican receives help - forgiveness
     (18:13-14)

Appendix G
Pastor's Weekly Preaching Calendar

Time	Monday	Tues.	Wed.	Thurs.	Fri.	Sat.
A.M. Sermon Preparation						
P.M. Counseling Admin.						
Evening Visitation						

Appendix H
Outlining a Sermon

TOPIC:

TEXT:

INTRODUCTION:
Purpose statement: to inform/ to convince/ to motivate.

I.   MAIN POINT:

II. MAIN POINT:

III. MAIN POINT:

Modify
Purpose
Statement

CONCLUSION:

Appendix I
Monthly Calendar

Month . . . . . . .199 . . . .

Date	Music	Sermon	Occasion, Purpose, Scripture, etc.
A.M. P.M.			
A.M. P.M.			
A.M. P.M.			
A.M. P.M.			
A.M. P.M.			

Monthly Calendar Sample

Month .SEP. 199 6.

Date		Music	Sermon	Occasion, Purpose, Scripture, etc.
1	A.M.	Special group	Joshua 1:1-9	Missions
	P.M.		No P.M. Church - Holiday	
8	A.M.		Canaan! God's best Joh 1:1-5	
	P.M.		Pulpit Guest	
15	A.M.	Theresa	Confidence Josh. 2:23-24	
	P.M.	Ron+Marie	5:1 Babylon Rev. 18:1-24	Communion
22	A.M.	Sharla+ Christa	Special guest	
	P.M.		Tribulation Rev. 18:1-24	
29	A.M.	Sharlotte	Ready to fight Josh. 2+3	Communion
	P.M.	Sharlotte	Israel in Prophecy Gal. 3	

Appendix J

Barber's and Boice's Sermons

Outlines from Dr. Barber:

Sermon 1

TOPIC: THE HIDING PLACE
TEXT: Numbers 35:14, 28
INTRODUCTION:
    a.) Corrie Ten Boom - book, song
    b.) Background - 48 Levitical cities; 6 cities of refuge, 3 on each side of the river.
    c.) Proposition - The city of refuge is a type of Christ.
    d.) **Application**: every Christian home should be a place of refuge. It should be a place of refuge for those seeking prayer and ministry.
    I.) THE CITIES OF REFUGE WERE ACCESSIBLE; SO IS JESUS.
    The cities were within running distance.
    II.) THE CITIES WERE DIVINELY APPOINTED, LIKE JESUS.
    a.) God appointed these cities.
    b.) Jesus was divinely appointed.
        1.) Religion is man-appointed
        2.) Jesus is God-appointed.
    III.) THE CITIES OF REFUGE PROVIDED SECURITY; SO DOES JESUS.

a.) The cities provided security for crime committed.

b.) Under the Blood of Jesus we are protected against guilt and the attacks of the devil.

IV.) A PERSON'S LIFE AND DEATH WERE DEPENDENT UPON THE HIGH PRIEST BEING ALIVE.

a.) Life was secured as long as the High Priest was alive.

b.) The Book of Hebrews tells us that Jesus our High Priest is alive, making intercession for us.

CONCLUSION:

Hymn: *And Can It Be*

Sermon 2

TOPIC: MIND-BOGGLING LOVE

TEXT: John 3:16

INTRODUCTION:

a.) Everyone's text.

b.) Three key words are: GOD, LOVED, and WORLD.

c.) Proposition - GOD, LOVED, and WORLD teach some valuable lessons.

What are the lessons that the key words in John 3:16 teach us?

I.) GOD—HERE WE HAVE THE MIND-BOGGLING PERSON.

What God?

a.) Not the gods of various religions of the world.

b.) It is a God who is capable of revealing Himself.

1.) The God of the Bible.

2.) The God with incommunicable and communicable attributes.

3.) The God of absolute power, wisdom, justice, perfection, wholeness, and felicity.

II.) LOVED—HERE WE HAVE THE MIND-BOGGLING ACTION.

"God loved the world"

a.) Different from the religions of the world.

b.) The Book of Hosea is an object lesson of His love.

III.) THE WORLD—HERE WE HAVE THE MIND-BOGGLING DIMENSION.

a.) No limits to God's love.

b.) No restrictions or conditions.

CONCLUSION:

GOD - the wonder of the Person. Perfection of all His attributes.

LOVED - the wonder of the action.

THE WORLD - everybody, needy.

- Notice the position of the word "loved," in the middle, linking God and world.

Outlines from Dr. Boice:

Sermon 1

TOPIC: THE ALL-SUFFICIENT CHRIST.

TEXT: Romans 11:35.

INTRODUCTION:

David's prayer of thanksgiving after receiving an offering for the temple forms the foundation of these verses and our study (Chronicles 29:10-14).

PROPOSITION:

The question in Romans 11:35 reminds us of the self-sufficiency, sovereignty, and independence of God.

What does Romans 11:35 teach about the all-sufficient Christ?

Consider the three rhetorical questions.

1 Chronicles 29:10-14 illustrates the text.

115

I.) ROMANS 11:35 TEACHES THAT OUR CONTRIBUTIONS EQUAL NOTHING

a.) We have nothing to contribute to our justification. We are justified by grace apart from human works.

b.) We have nothing to contribute to our sanctification. (The point of Romans 5-8.)

c.) We are chosen apart from works (Romans 9-11).

II.) ROMANS 11:35 TEACHES THAT WE CANNOT PUT GOD IN DEBT.

". . . that God should repay him"

We think we do when:

a.) We think we have caught God in some fault.

b.) We think we have been caught in an injustice.

c.) We think we have obligated God by some service.

CONCLUSION AND APPLICATION:

Romans 11:35 teaches that thankfulness and gratitude should be our response to the all-sufficient Christ.

a.) This text teaches about God's grace.

b.) We should respond in humility to God.

c.) We should respond in gratitude and love to the One who died for us.

d.) Our gratitude should lead to Christian service.

God is not obligated to give us anything, but He does so by grace.

Sermon 2

TOPIC: THE LIGHT OF THE WORLD[1]

TEXT: John 1:4-5.

INTRODUCTION:

The story of a Rhodesian missionary.

PROPOSITION:

John the Evangelist introduces the great image of Christ as the Light of the world to us in verses 4 and 5.

What does John mean when he declares that Jesus Christ is like light?

116

I.) LIKE LIGHT, JESUS IS REVEALED AS THE ONE WHO KNOWS GOD THE FATHER AND WHO MAKES HIM KNOWN

a.) God is pictured as light throughout the Old and New Testaments.

Illustration: Walter Chambers Smith's Hymn:

Immortal, invisible, God only wise,
In light invisible hid from our eyes,

Dr. E. M. Blacklock: "light penetrates all space."

b.) Light, like God, exists by itself.

II.) JESUS, LIKE LIGHT, EXPOSES THE WORKS OF DARKNESS

a.) The coming of Jesus exposes the world's darkness.

Illustration: Flash-light in a Christian Canadian camp.

b.) What is your reaction to Jesus, the Light?

Reject or accept Him and trust Him to remove your sins.

III.) JESUS, LIKE LIGHT, HAS NOT BEEN OVER-COME BY DARKNESS

". . . the light shines in the darkness and the darkness has never put it out" (Phillips).

What does "comprehend" mean?

It means "put it out," "to apprehend." Here the word means "to overtake,"—and by extension "to overtake in pursuit" or "to overcome"; compare John 12:35. It can also mean "to be overtaken, to be downed by one's opponent."

- What the physical darkness does each evening, spiritual darkness tried without success to do in the case of Jesus Christ.

Illustration: Malcolm Mugeridge coming to Christ, the Light.

CONCLUSION AND APPLICATION:

a.) Jesus is reflecting his light through us

". . . and the light shines in darkness."

1.) Christians are now the light; Christ is now reflected in us.

2.) We are lights simialr to John the Baptist.

b.) Do you see what Christ is saying? We are the light of the world when Christ shines through us.

c.) Do men see Christ in you?

d.) Is Jesus your light?

1.) Like light, Jesus puts confusion to flight.

2.) The light of Jesus is revealing and shining in your need of the Savior.

3.) If Jesus is your light, you will have guidance in the midst of darkness.

Sermon 3

TOPIC: THE UNIQUE CHRIST
TEXT: John 1:15-18
INTRODUCTION:
In French, John 3:16 is translated: "For God so loved the world that he gave his unique son." Unique means: "Being without a like or equal, single in kind or excellence, matchless."
PROPOSITION:
In verses 15-18, John describes four things that make Jesus unique:
I.) CHRIST IS UNIQUE IN HIS ORIGINS.

Vs. 15: "He that cometh after me is preferred before me: for he was before me."

a.) Here it is talking about existing before John the Baptist.

b.) He was one with the Father before he came to Earth.

Abraham saw Him in his day (John 8:56).

Isaiah saw Him (Isaiah 6:1-3).

c.) The New Testament often refers to the pre-existent Christ (Hebrews 1:1-2 and Philippians 2:5-8).

d.) Jesus was not a man only, but also the Son of God, always existing.

II.) CHRIST IS UNIQUE AS A CHANNEL OF GOD'S BLESSINGS.

Vs. 16: "And of his fullness have all we received, and grace for grace."

a.) This is talking about common grace: everything truly good that comes into your life—health, prosperity, knowledge, friendship, good times. Whatever it is, it comes from God.

Illustrated by the prophet and his harlot wife: a picture of God and us (Hosea 2:5, 8)

b.) All Christians are recipients of God's blessing through the person of our Lord Jesus Christ.

He satisfies our thirst and hunger. He is the Bread of Life and He is the Water of Life.

Illustration: John Newton's poem and a Keswick hymn.

III.) CHRIST IS UNIQUE AS THE SOURCE OF GRACE AND TRUTH.

Vs. 17: ". . . but grace and truth came by Jesus Christ."

The contrast is between law and grace.

In the law, righteousness came by works. In the New Testament, righteousness is based upon Christ and Christ's character.

IV.) CHRIST IS UNIQUE BECASUE HE IS THE ONLY ONE IN WHOM WE SEE GOD.

Vs. 18: ". . . no man hath seen God at any time; the only begotten Son, who is in the bosom of the Father, he hath declared him."

a.) The first part of the statement is universally accepted.

b.) Christ came in a way to make God known.

CONCLUSION AND APPLICATION:

What is your reaction to these things?

Do you know the truth of them personally?

You can know these things by faith in Jesus Christ.

---

[1] J. M. Boice, *The Gospel of John, Vol. I* (Grand Rapids: Zondervan Publishing House), pp. 50-57.

NOTES

NOTES

NOTES